The Genesis
of New Weapons

Pergamon Titles of Related Interest

 ON INTERNATIONAL POLITICS

The Genesis of New Weapons

Decision Making
for Military R & D

Edited by
Franklin A. Long
Judith Reppy

Pergamon Press

NEW YORK • OXFORD • TORONTO • SYDNEY • FRANKFURT • PARIS

Pergamon Press Offices:

U.S.A.	Pergamon Press Inc., Maxwell House, Fairview Park, Elmsford, New York 10523, U.S.A.
U.K.	Pergamon Press Ltd., Headington Hill Hall, Oxford OX3 OBW, England
CANADA	Pergamon of Canada, Ltd., Suite 104, 150 Consumers Road, Willowdale, Ontario M2J 1P9, Canada
AUSTRALIA	Pergamon Press (Aust.) Pty. Ltd., P.O. Box 544, Potts Point, NSW 2011, Australia
FRANCE	Pergamon Press SARL, 24 rue des Ecoles, 75240 Paris, Cedex 05, France
FEDERAL REPUBLIC OF GERMANY	Pergamon Press GmbH, Hammerweg 6, Postfach 1305, 6242 Kronberg/Taunus, Federal Republic of Germany

Library of Congress Cataloging in Publication Data

Main entry under title:

The Genesis of new weapons.

  (Pergamon policy studies)
  Bibliography: p.
  Includes index.
  1. Military research—United States—
Management. 2. Military research—Russia—
Management. I. Long, Franklin A., 1910-
II. Reppy, Judith, 1937-
U393.5.G46 1980   355'.07'0973   80-12243
ISBN 0-08-025973-1

Printed in the United States of America

Contents

Preface

The Peace Studies Program of Cornell University is an inter-disciplinary effort of teaching and research which is concerned with a better understanding of peace and war and with measures to reduce the likelihood of war and the costs of war should it come. Long term support for the program has come from the Ford Foundation as well as from the University.

In 1977 the Rockefeller Foundation made a grant to this program for a study by the co-editors of this book on the topic "U.S. Decision Making for Military R&D." This support has permitted a number of specific studies on the U.S. efforts in military R&D. In the central area of concern, that of the decision-making process for initiation and carrying out of R&D programs, it seemed important to obtain the views of some of the military officers, civilian managers of R&D programs and members of the research groups in industry that accomplish the R&D. An informal one day discussion meeting at the Aspen Institute in August 1978 brought together a small group of such experts and a most lively and productive discussion ensued. The success of this meeting suggested that it might be useful to organize a more formal workshop, with papers for discussion prepared in advance and distributed to the partici-pants. This workshop was held in New York on March 1-2, 1979. All of the topics that are presented in this book and a few additional ones were vigorously debated. The authors of the papers included in this volume then revised their papers in the light of the discussions and the editors went about the task of bringing them together as a book.

As editors, we owe heartfelt thanks to many people: the authors who prepared papers for discussion at the workshop; to the other workshop participants; the Rockefeller Foundation and the Cornell Peace Studies Program for their sponsor-ship and financial support. We are especially grateful to

Mrs. Deborah Ostrander for her help in organizing the workshop, and to Mrs. Lynn Ashworth for help in organizing the
papers and typing them in final form and for preparing the
index to the book. The subject of the book is important, and
we very much hope the analyses of this volume will be helpful
to the military and industrial groups that design and accomplish the U.S. programs of military R&D, to the congressional
and other groups with responsibility for their oversight, and,
not least, to the interested citizens who have concern about
what is a large, expensive and consequential part of the U.S.
military effort.

Franklin Long and Judith Reppy
Editors

The Genesis
of New Weapons

I

Introduction

1 Decision Making in Military R & D: An Introductory Overview

Franklin A. Long
Judith Reppy

For more than three decades expenditure for military research and development (R&D) has been by far the largest item in the R&D programs of the United States government. The initial impetus for this came from the many successful products of military R&D in World War II: rockets, radar, proximity fuses, anti-submarine devices, and, climactically, the atomic bomb. Most of the individuals involved in this wartime effort believed that science and technology would continue to be vital to the military. In his influential 1945 report, Science: The Endless Frontier, Vannevar Bush said, "In this war, it has become clear beyond all doubt that scientific research is absolutely essential to national security," and he urged a "permanent civilian activity to supplement the research of the [military] Services."(1) Reflecting a consensus on the importance of R&D, federal support for military R&D continued at a high level after 1945. The United States' strategic arsenal and many of today's conventional weapons are the result of this sustained effort to develop new military technology.

In recent years, funds for R&D programs have constituted 10 to 12 percent of the total U.S. military budget, or about $15 billion in fiscal year 1979. This figure represents 50 percent of total federal spending for research and development. More significantly, the spending for military R&D is a very large fraction of U.S. investment in military hardware, comprising 30 percent of total acquisition costs in 1979 (where acquisition is defined as the sum of R&D and procurement). Thus, spending for military R&D not only dominates the government's support of science and technology, but is also a disproportionate share of U.S. spending for military hardware - at least as judged by the standard of private firms, which typically spend only two to five percent of sales on R&D.

3

The standard justification for these large expenditures for military R&D is that they supply the new technology that the military services need and strongly demand. The Department of Defense is committed to a U.S. position of overall technical superiority in military technology; technical leadership is regarded as being essential in itself as well as being necessary to preclude technological surprise. Moreover, advanced technology is considered an area of comparative advantage for the United States, making it possible to rely on smaller numbers of superior weapons.

The substitution of quality for quantity has limits, however, and many military men have been dismayed by the small numbers purchased of some of the newest products of R&D purchased, such as the expensive aircraft and naval vessels. Since in real terms, funds for weapons acquisition have remained about constant, one might predict strong pressure from within the military to reduce the relatively large fraction of expenditures that currently goes to R&D. More generally, one might expect continuing concern and analysis of the proper balance between technological sophistication of new weapons and the quantities procured. But the quality-versus-quantity debate has had no apparent effect on the volume of resources allocated to military R&D.

A more profound question is, what is the overall impact of rapid changes in military technology on U.S. national security? Vannevar Bush was correct in saying that scientific research is essential to national security. But is it also true that more and more new military technology is better and better? Even apart from the cost, there are reasons for doubting that the answer to this is always yes. First, our principal adversary, the Soviet Union, appears committed to keeping closely abreast of the U.S. at all levels of military effort. Soviet capabilities for developing innovative military technology are, in general, considerably behind those of the U.S., but the Soviets have shown real ability to absorb new U.S. developments and move more rapidly to produce them for their own military forces.

These moves and countermoves in the development and adoption of military technology constitute an element of the arms race between the U.S. and USSR leading to escalating costs and higher potential for destruction on both sides, with only illusory gains in national security for either. A further problem is that the new technologies are rapidly taken up by other nations, typically by arms transfers, with a consequent world-wide buildup in levels and sophistication of armaments.

Another profound concern is the destabilizing potential of new military technologies. Both the U.S. and the USSR, and indeed most nations of the world, have a strong desire to avoid major war. Hence there is a general desire for weapons systems with a strong deterrence capability. But new military technologies can have a harmful effect on mutual deterrence in at least two ways. Some weapons systems are inherently destabilizing; for example, multiple warheads (MIRV) on strategic nuclear-armed missiles are destabilizing because they enhance the potential gain from, and hence the likelihood of, a nuclear "first strike."(2)   Other weapons systems, which may not be especially destabilizing, in the end are often so when first deployed by one side, because they upset a previous balance and introduce a new element of uncertainty about a future balance; long-range cruise missiles are currently leading to this sort of instability.   In sum, the rapid introduction of new military systems, which may appear uncontestably desirable as an element of "technological superiority," involves the risk of introducing undesirable destabilizing effects.   One cannot assume that military R&D is an uncomplicated good.

THE CORNELL/ROCKEFELLER WORKSHOP

The long-term goal of the Cornell studies on military R&D is to address these crucial issues of national security.   However, an essential first step is to understand in some depth how the U.S. programs of military R&D really work.   Only then can one hope to analyze and evaluate the connections between military requirements, R&D programs, the utility of new military systems, and their effects on national security. Where do research ideas come from?   Who evaluates them? How are choices made among them?   How are projects managed and carried out?   What are the roles of the military services, the civilian elements of the Department of Defense, and the industrial performers of R&D?   All of these questions are elements of decision making in military R&D.   We were therefore led to organize a workshop on this topic, which is of great interest in itself, and to solicit the participation of experts in the various aspects of the conduct of U.S. programs of military R&D.

The workshop, jointly sponsored by the Peace Studies Program of Cornell University and by the Rockefeller Foundation, was held in New York City on March 1 - 2, 1979.   The goal was to identify the chief actors and the important decision points in the development of new weapons.   A particular hope was to isolate and illuminate the factors that are involved in the initial stages of R&D projects; these early stages, which are the least visible and least well understood, appear to be the most important for determining the general character of U.S. military equipment.

The participants at the workshop included military planners and program managers, command officers from operation-

al military units, civilian analysts from within and without the
Department of Defense, persons from the defense industry,
and members of congressional-committee staffs. By including
representatives from the main organizational components involved in decision making for military R&D, we hoped to have
a lively discussion in which the main points of view would be
expressed. In this we succeeded; indeed, we could have
used much more time for discussion.

As the chapters of this book demonstrate, there is disagreement, even among a group of well-informed experts, on
some of the major issues raised by the military R&D program.
In particular, the general question, how well is the United
States doing? was answered rather optimistically by most of
those working within the R&D system, but much less favor-
ably by the outside analysts and those representing the military "customer." The questions of political control of military
R&D were also strongly debated, with differing views expressed on the appropriate relationship between the military
services and the Office of the Secretary of Defense (OSD),
and between the Department of Defense (DOD) and Congress.

We have grouped the chapters under four headings.
Those in the first group (Chapters 2-4) are broad, critical
assessments of the current U.S. procedures and institutions
for developing new weapons. These are followed by Alexander Kossiakoff's chapter (5), which traces in detail the formal
procedures for initiating a new weapons project in the Department of Defense. The chapters in the next group (6-8)
take up the comparison of the U.S. system for developing
new military technology with that of the Soviet Union. Here
the differences in the underlying "technology culture" are of
interest, as are the differences in organization and decision
making between the two countries. The last two chapters
discuss aspects of political control of weapons developments in
the United States: civilian control within the Department of
Defense, and program oversight and budgetary control by
Congress.

OVERVIEW OF THE MILITARY R&D PROGRAM

The scope of the U.S. program of military R&D is immense.
There are thousands of separate research projects, ranging
from the modest long-term research projects designed to
broaden the technology base, to major developmental efforts
for a new weapon or communication system. Virtually every
scientific and engineering discipline is represented. Project
size varies from very small to very large, and duration can
be from a few months to several years. Tables 1.1 and 1.2
present data on the main characteristics of the U.S. program.

The first table gives a complete accounting of total government spending on military R&D. The largest component is research, development, test, and evaluation (RDT&E) appropriation in the DOD budget, totaling $12.7 billion for fiscal year 1979. In addition to this sum, the Department of Energy spent about $1.1 billion on research related to nuclear weapons, and an additional $464 million was spent by the DOD on pay for military personnel assigned to the RDT&E effort but paid out of other appropriations. Finally, payments for independent-research and bid-and-proposal programs amounted to $1.106 billion; these are payments to defense companies for part of their costs for in-house R&D and proposal development; the costs are recovered by the companies as overhead charges against DOD contracts, and therefore do not appear separately in the DOD budget.(3)

Table 1.1. U.S. Government Funding for
Military R&D, FY 1979
(budget authority, est.)

	$ Billions
Department of Defense	
Research, Development, Test & Evaluation	12.699
Military Personnel Assigned to R&D	.464
DOD Payments for IR&D/B&P*	1.106
Department of Energy	
R&D on military systems	1.127
Total	$ 15.390

*Calendar 1978

Sources: National Science Foundation, April 1979, "An Analysis of Federal Funding by Budget Function, FY 1978-1980"; Department of Defense, "Annual Report on IR&D Costs and B&P Costs."

The sum of these categories was $15.4 billion for fiscal year 1979, a very large sum indeed. Table 1.2 gives four tabulations showing how the RDT&E portion of that total was spent: according to performer, to stage of development, to military service, and to budget activity. Apportionments at this level of aggregation are quite stable over time, and provide a good picture of some of the main features of the R&D

program.   First, the work is largely performed by private
industry, especially during the advanced-development and
engineering-development stages, during which prototypes are
built and tested, and component systems such as avionics are
integrated into the main weapons systems.   These stages usually absorb the bulk of the RDT&E funding, 56 percent in
fiscal year 1979 (Table 1.2, part B).   However, during the
late 1960s the largest category was operational-systems development, owing to the many modifications made to equipment
already in use in Vietnam, and the expensive "fixes" needed
for several large new systems that had continuing development problems after they had entered production (for example, the F-111 aircraft).   After 1970 the principal R&D efforts
shifted to new developments, such as new fighter aircraft for
the Navy and Air Force, new Army helicopters, and the
Trident submarine and missile.
       In recent years funding by service (Table 1.2, Part C)
has been remarkably stable, reflecting the realities of budgetary politics.   The relatively small share allocated to the
Army is the result of the absence of large, technically sophisticated systems in the Army's arsenal.   Aircraft and missiles are the two largest categories by weapon type in the
RDT&E budget, and these are categories in which the Army
has only a small R&D role.   The Navy and Air Force, sharing
the technologically demanding strategic missions, receive
almost equal shares of the R&D budget.
       Finally, the breakdown by budget activity in Part D of
Table 1.2 gives some sense of the RDT&E program emphasis
on new directions.   The science and technology programs
correspond to the spending in Part B for research and exploratory development, plus a portion of the advanced-development stage.   This can be thought of as DOD's long-run investment in the military-technology base; its size, one-fifth of
the total program, shows the seriousness of the pursuit of
continued technological superiority.
       These budgetary data sketch the overall composition of
the RDT&E program in the late 1970s.   Our current concern,
however, is with the individual decisions involved in selecting
and developing weapons systems, and in the choices which
lead to some weapons being developed rather than others.

DECISIONS FOR MILITARY
R&D: PROBLEMS AND PERSPECTIVES

The bulk of the United States' R&D effort, and the part
which is under analysis in the chapters of this book, is
undertaken in projects that have been initiated in response to
the stated operational needs of a military service.   The stated

Table 1.2.   Percentage Allocation of RDT&E;
FY 1979:   Various Categories

		Percent
A.	Allocation by Performer	
	Industry	69.8
	Government In-House	25.5
	Federal Contract Research Centers	1.9
	Universities	2.8
		100.0
B.	Allocation by Stage of Development	
	Research	3.7
	Exploratory Development	12.2
	Advanced Development	22.7
	Engineering Development	33.1
	Management and Support	11.0
	Operational Systems Development	17.3
		100.0
C.	Allocation by Military Service	
	Army	21.2
	Navy	35.4
	Air Force	36.0
	Defense Agencies/DT&E	7.4
		100.0
D.	Allocation by Budget Activity	
	Science and Technology Programs	19.9
	Strategic Programs	18.6
	Tactical Programs	41.6
	Intelligence and Communications	5.3
	Program-Wide Management & Support	14.6
		100.0

Source: DOD, The FY 1980 Department of Defense Program for Research Development and Acquisition, Statement by William J. Perry, Undersecretary of Defense, Research and Engineering.

need may have been developed in the field on the basis of some perceived operational problem, or it may have been stimulated by news of a promising new technology; in either case, the demand for the new capability will be translated into the language of a military requirement. The procedures that lead to the initiation of a military R&D project routinely call for a standard sequence of steps carried out by a single military service, with review and approval at specified "milestones" by the Office of the Secretary of Defense (OSD). The main steps during the early phases of the development cycle are formally described as follows:

- A statement of operational need by a military command
- In response, the formulation of a "mission element need" document, which typically calls for an R&D effort
- Validation by OSD of the requirement for a new development (Milestone 0)
- Analysis (done by in-house groups and/or by contract with industry) of alternative ways of meeting the mission need
- Selection of a limited number of options to be pursued (Milestone 1)
- Establishment of a project office to manage the new program
- Selection of industrial contractors to perform the development

The message in the chapters of this book, however, is that things are far more complex than this. Decisions on military R&D are embedded in a broader military and strategic context. Not just one service, but a unified command, is the real "customer"; international political factors as well as military utility enter into the definition of military needs. Decision making is carried out in well-established bureaucracies with ingrained interests and priorities. In chapters written from two differing perspectives, Admiral Gayler and Richard Garwin agree that the broader strategic context is frequently neglected because of bureaucratic and political pressures within the military services and in Congress. Both men complain of service parochialism, and Garwin, in particular, faults Congress for allowing parochial interests to dominate its overview of military programs.

It is not surprising that the separate military services with their own traditions and missions comprise a set of bureaucratic interest groups with competing definitions of the national interest. This is a familiar dilemma for organizations; in the case of military R&D, the effect is to reduce support within the services for new systems that threaten to replace established missions and weaponry, and also to make difficult the cooperative development and deployment of jointly used systems such as communications. Thus, the situation favors development along existing lines over more innovative solutions to military needs.

Jacques Gansler extends this point in his analysis, arguing that the oligopolistic structure of the U.S. defense industry reinforces the tendency of the military services to prefer incremental improvements in existing technological approaches for established missions. Technical elaboration by large engineering departments of the industry leads to over-engineered and overly costly products. Further, the acquisition process itself, with its bias toward firms with previous experience and its elaborate requirements for reporting, auditing, and record keeping, tends to exclude new firms, particularly small, innovative firms, from entering the defense market.

Taken together, these papers indict the current U.S. practices in military R&D for failing to encourage truly innovative ideas and carry out new developments rapidly. The result is lost opportunities, with delays and increased costs for the systems which are developed.

GENESIS OF NEW WEAPONS

In a more detailed examination of the decision process for initiating military R&D projects, Chapter 5 describes the crucial early stages of the development cycle. Kossiakoff is concerned with the progression from a stated operational need - whether long-standing or stimulated by a new technological opportunity or a change in the international environment - to a development project for a new weapon with specified characteristics. He puts particular emphasis on the role of the government R&D centers that supply much of the analysis in this early phase and perform a "bridging" function between the military, the technologists, and industry.

The step from state operational needs to a new R&D project is by no means automatic. The "need" may on analysis turn out to be unimportant, or existing military hardware may provide a satisfactory response. The R&D budget is not infinite, and choices must be made; a need may be real but of low priority. Even if the operational need is real and pressing, a complex analysis is usually required to decide which specific R&D project or projects would be the best response. For example, should the response be evolutionary, building on available technology, perhaps by modifying existing systems, or should it be revolutionary, building on some newly available science and technology?

The Department of Defense has devised elaborate procedures for analyzing these issues and reaching a decision

(see Figures 5.5 and 5.6 in Kossiakoff's chapter). Part of
the complexity of the procedures stems from the fact that
nearly everyone gets into the act - the operational groups of
the military, the technology specialists, the system analysts,
the comptrollers, and the representatives of the defense industry who hope to perform the R&D and ultimately to manufacture the product. Even when the outcome is a foregone
conclusion - for example, when a proposed program is known
to enjoy a high priority - the formal procedures must be com-
plied with. (The only exceptions are top-secret programs
which are managed in "black box" style, with knowledge restricted to very few persons.)

The requirement for consultation and review by a large
number of participants is aimed at ensuring comprehensive
coverage of all interested groups in an orderly way. This
feature of the decision making is, however, the focus of much
concern about program delays and about meddling by "outsiders" in program management. Just the coordination of the
program briefings in preparation for a decision milestone can
take weeks; the need to satisfy disparate interests can cause
further delay and may effect the substance of the programs
as well as the length of the development cycle. The need to
reach a consensus among a variety of participants undoubtedly tends to impart a conservative bias to the decisions and
make it more difficult to introduce innovative departures.
These costs must be balanced against the presumed benefits
which the formal procedures confer - namely, greater ration-
ality in decision making and the avoidance of costly mistakes - by forcing early scrutiny of mission need, expected
technical risks, and estimated life-cycle costs.

This emphasis on the formal requirements of the decision
process tends somewhat to obscure its real character. Where
concurrence by so many different offices is called for, one
can be sure that informal negotiations and bargaining take
place in advance of the formal decision points; it is in these
transactions that the institutional viewpoints of the services
and OSD are expressed and come to be embodied in new
weapons developments. For most systems, the basic technical
characteristics will be settled during the conceptual stage.
Thus, although the dollars spent during these stages are
small relative to later costs, the decisions made here affect all
that follows.

COMPARISONS OF U.S. AND USSR
MILITARY R&D

Research and development for military systems differs considerably from that for R&D for the civilian economy. The

end products of military R&D are highly specialized military
systems, and the R&D effort is usually done under a blanket
of secrecy. Although competition between research centers is
possible for military R&D, it is not very common, and competition at the production stage is even more rare. In spite of
these differences, the linkages between civilian and military
R&D are substantial and are fundamental to the progress of
the military side. The open, competitive programs of civilian
R&D in the U.S. provide most of the science base and much
of the technology base on which military R&D is built. Products of advanced civilian technology are routinely incorporated into military systems. For example, specialized electronics
devices developed by the civilian economy permit the military
to contemplate new technological solutions that might otherwise
not have been available.

At another level of comparison, it is probable also that
the process of weapons acquisition, including both R&D and
procurement, will be different in a statist economy like that
of the USSR than in a capitalist economy like that of the
U.S.   Comparison between the procedures for military R&D
of the United States and the Soviet Union is nevertheless of
great interest. First, because the USSR is the United States'
principal adversary and the only nation whose effort on military R&D is comparable to that of the U.S., the Americans
want to know how well the Soviets are doing relative to themselves. Second, Americans are interested in the strengths
and weaknesses of the Soviet structure for acquisition of military systems; they may have important things to learn from
it.

The three chapters in Part IV of this book deal with
these broad topics. Robert Perry writes on the U.S. "style"
of military R&D, and also analyzes how the U.S. procedures
have changed over the years and how well the U.S. is doing
currently. David Holloway discusses the Soviet style of R&D,
and Alexander Flax treats the influence of the civilian sector
of the economy on military R&D in both the U.S. and the
USSR.

The R&D procedures of the U.S. and USSR differ considerably. The Soviets do their military R&D in the separate
research institutes and design bureaus of the Ministry of Defense. The bureaus forward their designs to the manufacturing units of the Ministry at a comparatively late stage of
development. The armed forces of the USSR are involved in
setting operational requirements and in working with the R&D
design and production units, but their role appears to be less
central than that of the U.S. military services. This rather
different Soviet system seems to work well in designing follow-on systems for large series production and in developing
designs which lead to sturdy, effective military systems. It
seems to be much less effective in innovation, and the USSR

generally trails the U.S. in the development of new military
technology. However, the Soviet system has demonstrated
the ability to concentrate its resources on specific goals and
to organize and carry out intensive "catch-up" programs when
necessary.

Despite complaints that U.S. programs are insufficiently
innovative,   it is clear that, compared to the Soviet Union,
the U.S. is much more committed to searching for innovative
technology.   This is consistent with the U.S. commitment to
technological superiority.   However, it is also a reflection of
the fact that civilian science and technology is considerably
more advanced in the U.S.; as a consequence, more "building
blocks" of new technology are available to the military research groups in the U.S. than in the USSR.

This interrelation between civilian and military technologies is treated in considerable detail by Flax. His principal
thesis is that civilian science and technology cannot be dis-
joined from that for the military; nor should one wish to do
so; the civilian and military efforts interact with and support
each other.   There is some "spin-off" from military developments into civilian industry; reciprocally, there are large
flows of technological information from the civilian sector to
the military.   In this sense, the lower capability of Soviet
military R&D to yield innovations in military technology is
largely a reflection of the comparative lag of its civilian technology.   Flax agrees with Holloway, however, that the Soviets
have demonstrated impressive capabilities to organize and
manage concentrated "bit technology" efforts.

There has been a curious tendency in recent years for
many U.S. analysts to give good marks to the Soviet military
R&D program, even though its relatively inadequate capability
for innovation has been widely perceived.   Perhaps consistent
with this, there has also been a tendency to be critical
of many aspects of the U.S. military programs.   Thus, a
Summer 1977 study by the Defense Science Board of DOD concluded that "over the past 15-20 years the acquisition process
- from initial program concept to initial operational capability -
has increased in length by approximately 5 years on the
average," and the board identifies a number of planning
and procedural problems which plague the U.S. efforts.(4)

In view of the criticisms of U.S. programs of military
R&D and the charge that the situation has been growing
worse, not better, Robert Perry's conclusions are of considerable interest.   Perry examines the record of costs and
time-for-development for 32 major military systems that entered full-scale development during the 1970s.   During this
period three new management practices were emphasized -
hardware demonstration, performance testing, and hardware
competition - and each of them appears to have been beneficial.   A comparison of the overall results for these 32 pro-

grams with those from a similar study of an earlier group of
DOD programs leads Perry to conclude that on all counts the
1970 development programs did better than those of the
1960s.   Perry's optimistic summary is, "If the American military R&D style is difficult to categorize or define, it is at
least possible to suggest that outcomes have improved in recent years, that the process works reasonably well, and that
by all of the standards we can apply is increasingly effective."
It is important to note that Perry's research covered only the
full-scale development stage of the R&D cycle - which is,
however, the most costly stage.   Unfortunately, data are not
available for similar analyses of the predevelopment stages,
and, in the view of the Defense Science Board, it is these
stages that now take much longer times than previously.
There was much disagreement at the workshop with Perry's
optimistic conclusions about the trends in costs and development times, and one can conclude that the question of effectiveness and efficiency of the U.S. programs of military R&D
is far from settled.

ORGANIZATIONAL AND POLITICAL OVERSIGHT
FOR MILITARY R&D

An old Washington hand once said that whenever the federal
budget for a program rises above a billion dollars, congressmen will reach for their guns and take potshots at it.   Since
the proposed formal budget for RDT&E for the Department of
Defense in fiscal year 1980 is now $13.5 billion, one can be
sure that it will attract political concern and congressional
debate.   But the questions will be, or rather ought to be,
more than financial and political ones;   they should also concern the rationale of the military force structure and the objectives for the military in overall national security.
        Although there is a long tradition of civilian control of
the military in the United States, it has not often been effectively exercised in the somewhat specialized area of military
R&D.   Part of the problem lies in the continuing, probably
unavoidable, tension between the military who recommend and
manage and the civilians who approve and support the acquisition of military systems.   To quote Edwin Deagle,

> The central political feature of the weapon system
> acquisition process is that its control inevitably
> resides mainly in the hands of the services.   No
> one else in the system has the information and the
> financial and staff resources ... Moreover, no one
> can match the unique claim to control of the military
> requirements process that the wearing of a uniform

conveys. Thus the struggle for civilian influence
over the acquisition process will always be uphill.
And, given the differences and purposes among the
various political constituencies which surround the
Pentagon, civilian involvement will inevitably be
diffuse, fragmented, and pluralistic.

The political problem then is to ensure that the weapons-
acquisition process of military R&D and procurement reflects
wise choices and efficient procedures. Deagle argues that
much of the responsibility for this lies in the hands of the
secretary of defense and his staff, but that the secretary
cannot succeed in his task without responding to the complex
political cross-currents swirling through the Pentagon. A
logical organizational structure is helpful, but not enough,
says Deagle, "organization (and reorganization) is not a substitute for political leadership."

Political leadership comes from Congress as well as from
the executive branch. The important role of Congress in decision making for military R&D is the subject of the final
chapter. During recent years Congress has taken an increasingly active part in overseeing the programs and budgets of the Department of Defense; it has added committees
and expanded staff to accomplish this task. There are still
significant shortcomings, however. Faced with an RDT&E
program with thousands of individual projects, Congress has
not directed its attention to the rationale behind this multi-
tude of programs or to their implications for our overall military posture and national security. Traditional jurisdictional
lines between committees, and the competition of other responsibilities, divide and dilute congressional attention even
as the exigencies of electoral politics encourage intervention
in only a narrow range of programs with local impact. If
Congress is going to do more than stage a series of uncoordinated forays into the management of defense programs,
changes are needed to broaden the arena of public discussion
and to increase the incentives to members to engage in the
thoughtful and long-range oversight and decision making that
is their true responsibility.

LOOKING TO THE FUTURE

Several themes run through these essays on military R&D. In
the decision making on projects for weapons development,
there is a concern that the procedures for performing and
evaluating military R&D lead to lengthened development cycles, which in turn add to costs and deny needed capability
to military commanders. There is also a concern that the

bureaucratic interests of the military services and the large defense firms discourage innovative responses to military requirements. There is also a deep concern that the weapons developed should respond to real national-security needs, and that Congress should review the size and effectiveness of the R&D program in the context of the broadest possible definition of those needs.

The truth is that decision making on military systems is very difficult. There is little common ground between the development engineer convinced of the superiority of some new technical approach and the military commander faced with immediate problems of manpower, logistics support, training, and doctrine. Comparable gaps exist between the military services and the Pentagon planners: the one group is interested in responses to current threats: the other is trying to produce a balanced force structure for the future. It is not even clear, given the fortunate absence of a market test in the form of a major war, what the wise choices are.

Despite numerous reforms, the optimal procedures for making these choices remain elusive. Procedures which maximize the opportunity for review and evaluation by a broad range of participants run the risk of exacerbating problems of delay and cost. Alternatively, a shift to a more streamlined system might decrease the length and cost of the development cycle for individual programs, but perhaps at the price of increasing costs for the program as a whole because of a larger number of ill-conceived and costly failures.

What does seem clear is that more thoughtful attention needs to be paid to decisions on military R&D, placing them squarely in the context of overall national security. If U.S. goals and procedures for military R&D are to be changed in any substantial way, this will necessarily involve discussions at both the presidential and congressional levels. A first requisite will be a more clear understanding of the role of military forces in foreign affairs; following this, a better understanding of the structure of the U.S. military forces, not only in terms of personnel, but in numbers and kinds of weapons systems. What, for example, is the role of naval aircraft-carrier squadrons, and how many are needed? Also required will be a more clear resolution of the quality-versus-quantity debate, and hence a better understanding of the appropriate emphasis on new military technology. Besides these concerns with military utility, more analysis is needed within the decision making community on the dynamic effects of new military technology. Is there a race between the U.S. and the USSR for new military technology, and is the U.S. the principal innovator and spur for the race?

These discussions will involve many participants: the Department of Defense, the Office of Management and Budget, the Arms Control and Disarmament Agency, and the military

services, to name a few central ones. But the role of Congress will be crucial. Any new directions will necessarily
require congressional approval as part of the budget-making
process. But perhaps more importantly, congressional
hearings will be, or should be, principally where the pros
and cons of new directions will be given formal public presentation and analysis. In its committee structure and available staff, Congress has the tools for the job; what is less
certain is whether the requisite commitment exists. But unless the substantive issues are examined, and unless new
directions appropriate to the current and future problems are
developed and put in force, the U.S. will probably continue
to spend large amounts of money for military R&D that is
either not very essential or not very relevant.

NOTES

(1) Vannevar Bush, "Science: The Endless Frontier, A
     Report to the President" (Washington, D.C.: U.S. Gov-
     ernment Printing Office, 1945), pp. 12, 27.
(2) This destabilizing effect of MIRVs was vigorously ar-
     gued by non-military analysts in the late 1960s when the
     U.S. was considering their deployment. The arguments
     were not successful; MIRV systems are now deployed on
     both sides, and the destabilizing consequences have be-
     come painfully apparent.
(3) See Judith Reppy and Franklin A. Long, "The Pen-
     tagon's Program of IR&D: The Need for Reform," Bul-
     letin of The Atomic Scientists 32, no. 1 (1976): 30-36.
     To the extent that some of the IR&D/B&P costs are re-
     covered on contracts for RDT&E, there is a slight
     double-counting involved in the inclusion of all govern-
     ment payments for IR&D/B&P in Table 1.1.
(4) U.S. Department of Defense, Defense Science Board,
     "Report of the Acquisition Cycle Task Force," March 15,
     1978, pp. 1-4.

II

The Problems

2 Bureaucratic and Other Problems in Planning and Managing Military R & D*
Richard L. Garwin

Prescribing an optimum or even suitable military force is easier than achieving one, and paying for it does not guarantee
its existence. A rational approach would identify national
goals from which candidate missions could be derived. Consideration and investigation of existing elements and new
technology would allow definition of a number of options for
sub-forces, from which choices could be made best to fulfill
the missions. Not until the performance and cost of the options are known can the definition of mission actually be fixed: so iteration of the process shown in Figure 2.1 would be
required.

But even if all involved in the process were capable,
motivated, imbued with the national interest, unfettered by
tradition, and unaffected by political pork barrel or horse
trading, the process would still be very difficult because of

• the long life of the capital stock (ships, surveillance
  systems, and the like);
• the unknown nature of future threats (political, emerging military equipment and tactics); and
• limited resources.

There are a number of other major impediments, and
opinion may differ as to how fundamental they are:

• Attachment to old tactics and equipment (fighting the
  previous war)

---

*(A discussion paper for a Cornell-Rockefeller Workshop on
  Decision making for U.S. Programs of Military R&D, March
  1-2, 1979.)

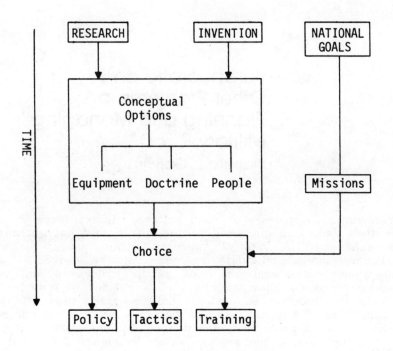

Fig. 2.1.   Idealized Flow Chart for
selecting new weapons systems

- Inadequate concern or flexibility in the choice of key personnel
- Political confusion between funds spent for defense and real defense capability
- The tendency to deny responsible decision makers appropriate options

    Before discussing in detail how these problems result from or influence deficiencies in the current R&D mechanism, or distort the options considered for future forces, we discuss some general aspects of military forces.

THE NATURE OF THE FORCES

To attempt to derive from the goals and values of this nation
a candidate set of missions for the armed forces would be
enlightening, but beyond the scope of this paper. Competitive efforts from a Joint Staff, from the Office of the Secretary of Defense, from schools of public policy and defense
analysis, might illuminate alternate mission sets and, for that
matter, alternative phrasings of national goals and values.
Several government studies over the last 20 years have
sought official statements of this type but found none, and
have been content to substitute their own. In general, such
analyses must deal with words like "freedom," "well-being,"
"God," "democracy," and "equality." They must choose a
level of assurance of survival and degree of proselytizing,
and choose the extent to which the "good guys" may use
force to prevail over their adversaries. In principle, R&D
decisions should take into account the missions as well as the
law of the land, including treaties.

As an example of broad missions, we note that navies
can of course fight navies - "fleet-on-fleet"; but in addition,
the United States has the task of securing its sea lines of
communication during peace and wartime; it may wish to use
the sea as a secure base from which to attack targets on
land; it may want to project national sovereignty to U.S. out-
posts, bases, or facilities, or to guide the evolution of international law and custom as in connection with the use of the
sea bottom.

In choosing military missions, the absence of a quantitative guide is no reason to avoid explicit discussion. Military
capability depends not only on equipment quality and quantity, but on policy, doctrine, tactics, personnel, training,
logistics, and the like. It is useful, if trite, to note that
overemphasis on one element, particularly hardware, will reduce capability within a fixed budget.

In prescribing a force to fulfill a stated mission, it is
conventional to compare "equal-capability forces" which will
then have a single measure of choice - cost. Emphasis on
maximum capability per platform - nuclear attack submarine,
aircraft carrier, guided-missile cruiser - is natural from the
viewpoint of the individual skipper, but such an approach can
seriously inhibit U.S. national capability to fight and win
against an opponent. Lanchester showed that the winning
power of a force under often-applicable circumstances is proportional to the effectiveness of each element times the square
of the number of elements. Thus units of one-fourth effectiveness need only be twice as numerous to match a nominal
force, and if there are four times as many units of one-fourth
effectiveness, the nominal force is wiped out after destroying
only about 13 percent of the opposing force.(1)

In comparing alternative forces, it is important to consider not only initial firepower but also durability, flexibility, and expandability in time of war. Unfortunately, defense R&D managers are typically much more interested in improving performance than in reducing cost, even though cost reduction may be much more important to military capability. Force options derive from a review of existing force elements as well as of technology available to provide new or improved elements. In the U.S. military, the tendency has been to use technology to improve unit capability, but our brief discussion of Lanchester's Law suggests that it is at least as important to use technology to reduce costs and to increase numbers of units of similar capability. The great success of consumer electronics and civilian computers derives at least as much from cost reduction as from performance improvement. Similarly, passenger aircraft have taken almost all the traffic from ships, not because of better amenities, but because of lower cost (including the passenger's time).

Not all technology is suitable for use in full combat. Aircraft, for instance, are very vulnerable and must be protected on airfields from mortar fire, which would little affect ordinary armored personnel carriers. Similarly, the very great cost reduction and performance improvement available with communications satellites and other uses of space may be difficult to preserve against a technologically advanced, determined enemy. R&D decisions must reflect these realities.

Furthermore, not all technology should be used to "improve" a force element. A case in point is that of the Trident submarine, which has a large nuclear plant to allow high speed, together with a 4,000-mile-range missile, and is about to be fitted with a 6,000-mile-range missile. The purpose of the high speed is not to provide security for the Trident on station, but to shorten the transit time from home port to the patrol area. This time, however, is already much shorter for a vessel equipped with Trident-1 missiles of 4,000-mile-range than with Poseidon missiles of 2,500-mile-range, and there is every reason to believe that U.S. security would have been improved by the use of a reactor plant in Trident of half the present power or less. Thus, technology must be chosen judiciously. A dollar spent unnecessarily is a dollar of military capability denied us. Worse, the rationalization and arguments which support the unnecessary expenditure can contaminate the national security discourse for years.

THE NATURE OF BUREAUCRATIC AND OTHER PROBLEMS

Our purpose here requires a more general and less technical examination of problems of military capability and R&D, an

examination which goes well beyond any search for technical
fixes to such specific problems as the defense of Minuteman
silos, improving radar satellites, substitution of liftfans for
large tails on STOL aircraft, and the like. Nor shall I complain here that people are not smart enough to predict the
future, or that there are smart enough people but they are
not in the Defense Department, that we have insufficient
funds, that materials do not exist with the right properties to
do the task, and so on.

Our concern, instead, will be whether the structure of
the Defense Department, of the administration, or of the
bureaucracy as a whole substantially reduces the efficiency
and the effectiveness with which we pursue national security
goals, without at the same time compensating by avoiding
errors and excesses. Finally, we ask whether feasible modifications in process or structure could lead to significant
improvements.

The Role of the Congress

There is much room for improvement in the procedures and
the influence of the Congress on the R&D process and on
military capability in general. Although the number and
quality of those staffs in the Congress concerned with national security and research and development have increased
greatly over the last decade, congressional procedures and
influence are still such as to result in often irresponsible and
harmful actions.

In some cases this is due to genuine ignorance or mis-
understandng on the part of a member of Congress or of his
or her staff. At times it is due to constituent pressures,
particularly organized constituents such as corporations wanting contracts for the continued production of, say, aircraft
or submarines. At times the pressures come from localities
and groups of voters seeking federal expenditures in their
region; at times, from some congressional staff or member
with some favored technology in energy, military shipping,
transportation, or the like. Naturally the Congress cannot be
expected to repeat all of the analysis which has entered into
the administration's decision making and the recommendations
of the Defense Department. Nor should one desire or expect
the Congress to be a rubber stamp on the administration's
request. What is needed is congressional review and action
to provide effective military capability now, and, at least as
important, to provide the incentives for the administration to
do its job better in the future.

Unfortunately, my observation is that congressional procedures too often reward dishonesty and lack of candor in
program presentation, penalize tightly reasoned arguments

and tightly structured programs, and impede the effectiveness of administration officials concerned with national-security affairs, making it increasingly difficult to bring such people into the government or to retain them and make good use of their talents and experience. There is an absence of both law and custom in regulating the actions and influence of the Congress. It has been recommended that, rather than to provide good answers, the proper function of the Congress is to ask questions and to insist on respectable answers and alternatives from the administration.(2) Such responses must of necessity call forth greater awareness of alternatives at lower levels in the administration and must provide for better understanding of relative capabilities, costs, survivability, and other such factors.

A member of Congress supporting the B-1 bomber, the principal contractor of which is in his district, may have a better understanding than his colleagues of the strategic threat and the possible options available to the United States, and he may have come to the conclusion that the best re- sponse for the nation would be to buy the B-1. On the other hand, so long as members in general explicitly or implicitly place such importance on reflecting the views of their constit- uencies, one might imagine that it is this which motivates the conviction and energy of the member in his support of the B-1. The result of these attitudes and actions on the part of the Congress, is, in my opinion, a perhaps-warranted belief on the part of the officials in the executive branch that it is pretty much useless to do a good job in proposing a program and that it is best to ask for more than one needs, to spend all that one gets, to propose programs which are most readily supported by politically attractive arguments, and to choose programs which have direct benefits to the districts of impor- tant members over programs which may benefit the entire nation.

I have placed first the role of the Congress because I find it to be the origin of much that is wrong in R&D decision making and also to be an impediment to correction.

The Influence of the Five-Year Defense Plan

I welcomed the introduction in the McNamara era of the Five- Year Defense Plan (FYDP) which formalized a process that was necessary and common in business and replaced the more usual annual budget analysis and planning. Of course, any planner and budgeter knows that a five-year plan sets a direction and a rate of which only the first year or so is firm. Thus, the subsequent years in the plan may require more funds, or a program may be terminated before reaching those years. Furthermore, every year new programs will be started which are not imagined at the beginning of the FYDP. Thus a "wedge" must be left in the FYDP to accommodate these new programs, and as one looks ahead, one must make room for the fruits of the R&D to enter into the more costly full-scale development, procurement, and operation.

While the FYDP has introduced a considerable amount of discipline into the armed services and the Department of Defense (DOD) as a whole, the Office of Management and Budget (OMB) and the president are much more concerned with the current and next year's budget. Too often, in trying to manage a deficit or create a surplus, OMB will pay an exorbitant price in military capability or future expenditures to move funds from the fiscal year under consideration into some later year. This tendency is then reflected among planners in DOD in the choice of programs which may be considerably more expensive in resource expenditure on an overall dollar basis (and may be much more expensive even on the basis of discounted present value - DPV) in order to obtain approval of and commitments to programs which are felt desirable. This has two effects: it mortgages the future expenditure of the Defense Department, and it may distort the choice among programs to the detriment of those possibly more desirable.

In regard to the FYDP, five years is a very short time in the development cycle, and especially in the overall life cycle of many programs, including strategic systems, major intelligence systems, and the like. Thus, two programs which may be equal in capability at every year in the future, and which have comparable five-year costs, may differ considerably in ten-year costs and may differ by even more in the life-cycle cost projection. Thus, if Program X has a five-year cost of $500 million and Program Y a five-year cost of $600 million, the choice between them, considering just the FYDP, might be made on other grounds (the difference in estimated cost being relatively small and uncertain). One should, however, be fully aware of the possibility that Program X may have only a $600 million ten-year cost while Program Y has an $1,100 million ten-year cost, presenting an entirely different problem of choice in the face of continuing necessity for economy in defense expenditures.

Thus, while the FYDP imposes some discipline, it is by no means enough to ensure fully rational decision making in the Defense Department or in OMB. My own experience is that although life-cycle cost or at least ten-year costs are indeed reviewed at the level of the Undersecretary of Defense Research and Engineering, and perhaps at the level of the Secretary of Defense, it is extremely difficult in comparative program analysis to obtain ten-year cost projections, even when the comparison can be very significant, as in the example chosen.

It is even more difficult to obtain discounted-present-value comparisons of the various streams of expenditures and benefits. It seems to me that DOD has done an inadequate job of mandating, for planning purposes, a universal procedure (or procedures) for determining DPV. I would advocate the use of a discount rate in this highly technological area on the order of 5 percent per year net of inflation. Another might choose a different inflation-free discount rate, ranging from 2 to 10 percent annually; but if this is important, then the use of some discount rate is even more important, and a specific figure ought to be mandated by the Office of the Secretary of Defense after an appropriate brief study. Note that the discount rate is set by the bulk of alternative expenditures and not by the particular program under discussion. I fully realize the limitations of data and analysis available to define the appropriate discount rate, but the foundation will improve as more emphasis is placed on this tool.

Non-Weapons Programs

I have already mentioned the difficulty which one has in initiating a new program in a defined field in competition with the continuation of an existing program. Naturally, the manufacturer of the F-4 fighter aircraft did not want to see that production terminated in favor of a new F-15, unless the F-4 manufacturer expected to receive the F-15 contract or a substantial fraction of that work. Similarly, those interested in the Trident submarine program would be reluctant to see the SLBM mission carried out for a small fraction of the cost by a new production system that involved the termination of the Trident procurement. There are more people strongly interested in fostering large expenditures for given military capabilities than for devising less costly alternatives, and there is no competitive race between defense departments in the United States such as those that, in principle, lower costs in the market for home food processors, pocket calculators, and ball-point pens. Nor is it common to find among Defense Department officials an awareness that the money they spend is as important as if it were their own. This view is evidenced by the end-of-year panic to spend dollars lest they evaporate and be unavailable, a syndrome known to all government contractors and even to many in the private sector. Difficult as it may be to replace an existing production line with new development (and difficult even to initiate development at a low level, because of its virtual threat to terminate production of the existing system), it is even more difficult under the usual planning regime to initiate a non-weapons system which would improve the capability of a considerable number of weapon systems. A case in point is the

Global Positioning System, GPS, a set of 24 satellites broad-casting microwave radio signals, which, by reception on an appropriate receiver-computer anywhere in the world, will give location of that receiver in three dimensions to an accu-racy of 10 meters every 0.1 seconds. Accurate velocity in-formation in three dimensions is also available from the sys-tem. Throughout the 1960s, GPS faced extreme difficulties in initiation and funding, although it clearly had the promise of greatly increasing the capability for bombardment of ground targets by replacing and improving existing navigation sys-tems on aircraft and by its use in guiding bombs, shells, and missiles all the way to their targets. Furthermore, by re-placement of much more expensive and less accurate LORAN and OMEGA navigation systems, there were substantial opera-tional and safety benefits to be associated with GPS. Finally, the deployment of the system for use by the military would provide a navigation system for use by the civil sector (such as in airlines, shipping, private vehicles, and search and rescue) of unprecedented accuracy.

So far as I know, in the decision procedure for the Global Positioning System, no attention was paid to the bene-fits which would accrue to the civilian sector. Further com-plicating the decision was the competition between Navy tech-nology and orbits, and Air Force technology and orbits, which was comprised by the use of Air Force signals and Navy orbits (in my opinion, just the wrong decision, when one considers the much larger expenditure on ground equip-ment and the considerable delay in the availability of 24-hour continuous positioning data as the system was being de-ployed).

I remember a 1970 meeting in the basement of the Penta-gon, at which the Navy particpant was asked to provide $50 million for the development of GPS. His response was that the Navy was already $500 million short in next year's ship-building budget and would spend the money there rather than on GPS. That not one of the ships so funded would provide any military capability before GPS could enhance the perfor-mance of every ship appeared to have little weight. In short, there was no bureaucracy for the development of a lower-cost replacement for existing navigation systems, an improvement in capability which would allow reduction in the number of aircraft in the fleet and a reduction in training time and complexity of those vehicles, and which would pro-vide substantial safety benefits throughout the services as well as a much-needed precision-positioning capability for ground patrols, artillery, and the like.

Cross-Bureaucracy Problems

Defense R&D bureaucracy is hardly unique in protecting its
turf, resisting innovation and competition; the same behavior
is found in industry and in the professions. But the consequences of these common failings can be more catastrophic in
the case of defense R&D. For example, in the face of growing Minuteman vulnerability to Soviet ICBMs, the best solution
may well be the use of minisubmersibles of perhaps 350-ton
displacement, deployed near U.S. shores and each carrying a
number of long range ICBMs outside the pressure hull, hori-
zontally disposed and in appropriate containers. But the
United States Air Force is unfamiliar with the development
and operation of submarines, and appears loath to tread on
the turf of the United States Navy. The latter is engaged in
arguments to support and continue the Trident submarine
building program (although if that program were proposed ab
initio, the Navy would probably not choose it in comparison
with a smaller stragic submarine). As it is, to endorse the
minisubmersible as a near-term option would mean that the
Navy was prejudicing the continuation of the Trident program; this cannot be expected to happen.
    Even the analysis of the promise of minisubmersibles is
substantially impeded by this cross-bureaucracy problem.
This could be obviated by the provision of study funds from
the Advanced Research Projects Agency of DOD or from the
Office of the Secretary of Defense, but even this solution is
no panacea, since organizations which derive most of their
funds in contracts from the United States Air Force or the
United States Navy are reluctant to imperil their future by
accepting modest study contracts whose success may expose
to criticism or termination large programs that are important
to their chief sponsors. Indeed, there is evidence that the
minisubmersible has previously been found attractive, but
that further analysis and exploratory work has been terminated for just the stated reason.

Government Program and Policy Leadership

There is a serious problem regarding individuals who determine policy and lead programs, one which seems insoluble
under the democratic system. An administration brings in
new people to fill the top positions, many of whom have had
no contact with that function before; those who have, may be
considerably out of date in their understanding of the problems. In the time required for these new people to begin to
function, those in the second and third echelon (civil ser-
vants in the Department of Defense) essentially make the
decisions and determine policy. Thus, there is a substantial

degree of coherence in direction from one administration to the next, even in cases in which the new administration has campaigned and won by challenging the policy and programs of the old.

This is familiar in the B-1 controversy, in the continuity in programs to achieve hard-target kill capabilities for our ICBM force, and the like: individuals who were instrumental in advancing such policies in the Nixon-Ford administration still occupied positions of power in directing and contracting for studies in the Carter administration. Furthermore, such individuals may form part of an informal clique, with substantial communication to and from congressional staff and members, the press, industry, and others. Thus it is not simply a matter of a civil servant doing his best on the job to follow the policy of the current administration; previously-made policy decisions tend to carry on even when a new administration expects changes to be made.

The remedy for this problem is more difficult to state than the problem itself. The best I can offer is to make the decision process more open within the administration - that is, to those with adequate security clearance who may participate in the development of options. Thus, the final papers which go to the Secretary of Defense or even to the President ought to be available to such people for comments to ensure that they fairly represent the arguments that have been prepared at the lower levels. Unfortunately, such papers have a good deal of sensitivity, and unscrupulous individuals could leak them to newspapers or to industry, which could instigate challenge during the congressional debate, or the like. It is these latter tactics which cause presidents and secretaries of defense to limit access so sharply to papers prepared for their decision.

CONCLUDING REMARKS

This chapter has addressed the bureaucratic and other problems affecting defense R&D decision making. Of course, in addition to these problems there are the truly substantive ones (which I eschewed discussing in my introduction) of insufficient knowledge, inadequate preparation, insufficient tools, and the uncertainty of the future. But unless the bureaucratic problems are recognized and conquered by organization, leadership, and particularly by the improvement of the role of the Congress, large portions of the vast sums we spend on defense will be wasted.

NOTES

(1) This follows simply from the observation that a force of
     equal initial firepower overall (but fewer platforms) can
     absorb fewer hits before being destroyed.   See S. W.
     Lanchester, Aircraft in Warfare (London: Constable and
     Co., 1916).
(2) Committee   for   Economic   Development,   Research   and
     Policy Committee, "Congressional Decision Making for
     National Security," September 1974.

3 Decision Making in Military R & D

Noel Gayler

To speak of R&D decision making "within the services" is to foster an illusion that major R&D decisions are made, can be made, or should be made within a single military service. Quite the contrary is the case. The services usually propose, but quite a constellation of others dispose. So a full discussion of the service role requires at least a summary description of the total process in which it is imbedded or entangled.

We can see a number of factors in the evolution of R&D decisions:

- U.S. perception of its role in the developing world
- U.S. conception of the role of military power in that place - or, more directly, in its survival
- An estimate of the importance of military technology to military power
- A notion of how best to develop military technology that is relevant and useful

Very dedicated, experienced, and talented people, inside and outside the armed services, have worked on these problems. Some of the very best are working on them now. Yet there is a general feeling of dissatisfaction with results. This chapter will argue that our difficulties are principally institutional and perceptual, not operational or technical, and that there are remedies.

GENERAL STRATEGIC SITUATION AND THE
REQUIREMENTS PROCESS

The U.S., still the most prosperous nation in the world, be-
lieves itself to be benign and compassionate, bringing together democratic values and economic progress to share and encourage in the world. It is not so regarded everywhere. On
the one side is a major and thrusting military power, the
USSR, whose ambitions are clearly inimical to those of the
U.S. On the other, there is a great array of developing na-
tion-states who have in common, in varying degree, three
characteristics: they are in want; they are politically and
economically undeveloped; and they seek an external focus for
their resentments.

     We see clearly the political and moral necessity for the
U.S. to help the underdeveloped world. With less agreement,
we see the necessity of the U.S. treating with the USSR in a
way that is firm but nonprovocative. With overwhelming consensus, we believe that U.S. military power is essential to
the peaceful evolution of a better world, and to its own survival. There is much less consensus on how military power is
to be integrated with economic power and diplomatic intiation.

     What has all of this to do with service decision making?
Simply, within the military services, even more than outside,
the strategic context is important in the definition of requirements. Some military professionals have spent a working life
examining these premises. Almost all carry some part of them
in their military background.

     In a logical world, the initiation of a military develop-
ment follows from the confluence of a military need and a
technical opportunity. Ideally, the process would be iterated
many times, from basic concept to detailed development. The
operator, or "customer," cannot define what he really wants
until he has a clear understanding of what he can have -
technically, fiscally, politically, and practically. The developer, or "provider," cannot specify his product without a
clear understanding of the purpose and context of its potential use. This association of customer and provider should be
an intimate fast-acting servo-loop. It is not.

     The services enjoy a dominant position in the statement
of military requirements. They write the "first draft," based
on the most experience, usually on considerable technical
competence, and on the most homework. They can be powerful and single-minded advocates. They are seen as both customer and provider, and as the ultimate judges of "purely
military" worth. In most respects, they are well qualified,
and in many instances, effective.

     Yet there are important weaknesses:

- The services are no longer the real military customer; the unified commander is. The Navy can no longer be solely responsible for sea control, nor the Air Force for aerospace, nor the Army for the ground battle. Each is vitally dependent on the others, and this is reflected in the unified command system - but not in the requirements process.
- The services have institutional viewpoints. The Navy sees control of the sea routes as essential to the Oceanic Alliance, as indeed it is. The Air Force sees aerospace use and control as essential to military power, as indeed it is. The Army and the Marine Corps see control of ground as the ultimate determinant of battle, and this too is correct. Melding of these points of view into a coherent whole, if it takes place at all, has to take place at a higher review level.
- There is a general, though not universal, bias for improvement of contemporary weapons systems rather than development of revolutionary ones. There is a powerful constituency in the Army for manned armor and artillery; within the Air Force, for manned bombers and tactical aircraft; within the Navy, for destroyers and submarines and aircraft carriers. "Improvements" mean generally bigger and better and more expensive items in an inexorable advance toward the white elephant. We look backward clearly to the patent necessity to replace horse cavalry and the battleship; we see forward less clearly.
- There is no single-service basis for the adequate support of developments serving a broad spectrum of military needs. Some examples are space vehicles, electronic warfare, C4 (command, control, communications, computers), and logistics.
- The services are not well equipped to deal with such questions as arms control and inhibited weapons.
- They share in acute fashion the Washington syndrome of short-term living. It is very difficult to concentrate on the future when your throat may be cut fiscally tomorrow.
- There are simply too many people in the act, and the services are well aware of the political imperatives if any program is to survive. The result is an insensible but real distortion from what is needed to what can be sold, or to what must be preserved as something better than nothing.

TIME, TECHNOLOGY AND PROCUREMENT

The services execute most development programs, but they have only fragmented control over time and little more over technology and procurement practice. There is apparently not much recognition of the value of time, or conversely of the cost of delay, in the development and procurement of weapons systems. A cost-versus-time chart for a typical idealized development program looks like Figure 3.1. A very fast program costs a little more, owing to redundant parallel approaches, overtime, materials premiums, and other reasons.

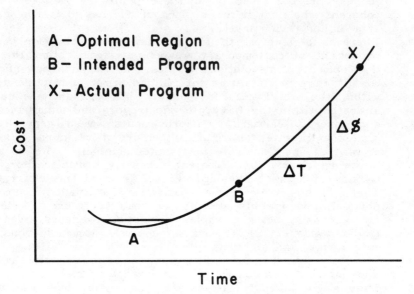

Fig. 3.1.   Cost versus time for a
weapon systems development.

There is a broad range of optimum development time (region A in Figure 3.1) where development is both cheapest and most reliable. We generally plan to develop at some point like B, where time is longer and costs are higher, but the program at least looks feasible. And we end up making changes, usually in response to fiscal stringency. Each change costs time and money, and we finish by operating at point X. Sometimes we get so far up on the asymptotic curve that nothing at all comes out - the technology is obsolete or the requirements have changed in the meantime. My intuition is that the U.S. takes twice as long and spends twice as much on the representative military development as it should.

Nor is this all. In most tactical systems, the value of the entire system is a strong function of its technological capability to do a military job - to track submarines, silence artillery, shoot down aircraft, or whatever. But the adversary is improving too, and this technical edge is a diminishing asset. A project starts existence at the time that a requirement is fully understood and the relevant technology is available, and it ends useful existence at the time it is obsolete, when it can no longer do the job. The useful life, however, is only that time when it is in the field. If we take a great deal of time over project approval, a long time to develop, a long time to procure and field, we have a short useful service life before obsolescence. Conversely, if we make up our minds, develop and procure at an optimum rate, and field promptly, we have a long useful life. But the entire system cost has got to be amortized (subject to some minor adjustments) over the useful service life, not the entire project life. Here, too, the U.S. may be paying twice what it should for what it gets. Apparent prudence can be costly and dangerous. The proof of this pudding lies perhaps in the conspicuous example of some extremely successful projects which telescoped or omitted the normal processes of review and delay.

SOME MODEST PROPOSALS

The technical differences that once distinguished ship from tank (or horse) and from plane have all but disappeared. Missiles, aircraft, helicopters, and surface-effect ships share aerospace technology. Electronics is service color-blind, as are computer technology, space, communications, or (nearly) weapons. The more prosaic beans and bullets and bedding have always been so, or should have been. The development and procurement of these systems and articles by individual services is an anachronism that is increasingly costly both in money and in effectiveness.

I make no specific organizational proposals here, but venture some principles:

- Procurement in common, except for clearly unique equipment such as submarines, battle tanks, and heavy strategic and transport aircraft
- Responsiveness to <u>functional</u> warfare <u>needs</u>; for example, space control, sea control, land battle, tactical firepower, long-range transport, C3I
- Responsiveness, within resources, to operational commanders
- Decentralization consistent with effectiveness

It is worth warning that the great gains from consoli-dated procurement may be more than offset by loss if the procurement system grows too big and too independent. A certain amount of intended competition may be necessary and efficient. There is grave danger that a procurement organi-zation may become too big to be manageable. Without safe-guards, procurement can become an end in itself to those engaged in it. It should instead be carefully organized to be responsive to the authoritative policy directive of operational commanders in the satisfaction of their requirements. The obvious solution is to decentralize along functional lines - but with great care to avoid losing policy control or technical synergism.

Second, the U.S. should recognize its unified operating commanders, not its services, as the military customers. The military customers are appropriately brought together by the Joint Chiefs of Staff.

Third, the U.S. should reduce the innumerable people in the act to one level of initiation (customer and provider), one level of review in the Department of Defense (Office of the Secretary of Defense), one more in the executive branch (Office of Management and Budget), and one in the Congress (ideally, a single committee in each branch). Organization alone cannot remedy all deficiencies or exploit all opportun-ities. It can, however, facilitate and clarify responsibility.

I should make clear that none of the above is a sug-gestion for the amalgamation of the services. The special expertise and morale of combat pilot, tanker, submariner, artilleryman, marine, indeed all the military specialties, are priceless military assets, nurtured and fostered by identifica-tion with their service. Nor do I believe that technology and material are necessarily or even usually dominant in military strength. Lanchester's laws have been broken more often than followed in real battle. More often than not, the im-ponderables of leadership, morale, intelligence, and will have carried the day. It usually makes more difference who has the smartest general or admiral and the bravest and best trained troops than who has the smartest weapons system. But still, the technology does and will continue to make a difference. For the first time in our modern lives, the U.S. is up against a potential adversary who has more than it has.

4 The Defense Industry's Role in Military R & D Decision Making
Jacques S. Gansler

That the defense industry influences decision making in the Department of Defense is almost a truism. One could discuss profit motives and marketing efforts, but these are present in any supply-and-demand environment. To understand truly the role of the defense industry in military R&D decision making, it is necessary to look at the structure of the defense industry and at the way in which the DOD does business - particularly the influence that DOD business practices have on the structure of the defense industry. In my opinion, these, together with the structure of the DOD itself, are the forces that shape decision making in military R&D.(1)

The defense industry structure and the process of government acquisition are not independent; in fact, they are mutually reinforcing; nor are they separate from the internal institutional or structural characteristics of the DOD itself. Together, these three aspects of the defense marketplace (namely, the supply and demand structures, and their interacting through the acquisition process) result in the defense R&D programs which exist today. This chapter will only address the first two of these factors, since the third is addressed in other chapters of this book.

It is the thesis of this chapter that the market is dominated by a few large, vertically integrated firms, and that this structure presents very large "barriers to entry" for small firms and commercially-oriented firms. When these characteristics are combined with the acquisition process - long development times, sole-source production awards tied to R&D contracts, large program uncertainty, cyclical budget variations, little if any consideration of a viable industrial base (rather, treating each program on its own), and many other unique and restricting practices - the overall effect is an R&D program that emphasizes low risk, tradition-oriented lines. The focus is on innovation (product improvements) rather than new inventions, and on quantitative changes ("more of the same") rather than significant qualitative changes (in totally new directions). Finally, an inordinate amount of DOD research-and-development dollars are spent on "routine" engineering functions associated with full-scale development of weapons systems and engineering changes during production, instead of more of the R&D budget being spent on new system concepts and critical-element-feasibility demonstrations.

Most of these problems have been recognized for some time, but little has been done to address their basic causes in the structure of the defense industry. What is particularly troublesome is that in recent years the trend in U.S. military R&D has been going in the wrong direction, along the following lines:

- Rising unit-production costs, which are being "designed into" each new generation of equipment
- Increasing costs of R&D itself, especially of full-scale development
- Far longer acquisition cycles
- Increasing overhead burdens, including the larger costs of proposals
- Less real competition for most of the DOD dollars, especially for production programs
- Less component R&D - the critical base of all systems
- Far fewer component suppliers (the low-volume, low-profit, specialized business is unattractive)
- Increasing vertical integration, including through acquisition
- Increasing institutional inertia to nontraditional ideas
- Weakening of a clear U.S. technological leadership position
- Increasing "buy-ins" for the few available R&D programs

In general, while technological evolution is increasing at a steadily more rapid rate, the DOD's R&D programs are being increasingly stretched out, held up for decision making, impeded by increased institutional inertia, and are not using new technology to lower the costs of systems - as is done in the civilian world. Thus, things are getting worse. Considering the long response time of so large an institution as the DOD, immediate action is required.

It is the conclusion of this chapter that significant structural and procedural changes must take place in order to improve the efficiency and effectiveness of the decision-making process in U.S. military R&D. To have maximum impact, these changes must address all three measures of R&D

effectiveness; namely, (1) development of the most useful type of equipment, (2) getting more military capability (quantity and quality) for the acquisition dollars available, and (3) managing each program within the approved program resources. Some of the areas for change include institutional emphasis on: nontraditional missions and equipment; qualitative changes; integration of commercial and military work; greater stability in the R&D labor force; more technology demonstration, especially of components and subsystems; greatly improved economic efficiency of full-scale development programs; less competition on initial research and development awards, but continuous competition on follow-ups in R&D and into production; far shorter overall acquisition cycles; more separation of research and development from production; maintenance of U.S. technological leadership while achieving NATO standardization; and greater emphasis on the use of technology for cost reduction, along with performance improvements.

THE IMPACT OF THE INDUSTRIAL STRUCTURE

When one thinks of the U.S. defense-industry structure, some of the characteristics which immediately come to mind are:

- High concentration - a few large firms
- Emphasis on technology - from management through the labor force
- Vertical integration - both from parts through systems, and from R&D through production
- Very high "barriers to entry" - difficult for new firms to enter the business
- Distinct "dual economy" consisting of prime contractors and lower-tier contractors

Let us consider each of these, and its influence on the military R&D decision process.

Clearly, defense is a highly concentrated industry. For example, in fiscal year 1977 eight companies(2) accounted for approximately 45 percent of the dollars spent on defense research and development.(3) What causes this concentration, and how does this concentration affect military R&D decision making? Scherer has pointed out that the more concentrated markets are, the more intensely R&D is encouraged by the firms involved.(4) However, more recent data show questionable correlation between concentration ratios and the amount of R&D spending. In any case, in the defense industry most R&D is government funded, and the DOD has been successful in its desire, in the post-World War II era, to increase the emphasis on the R&D area. (Since 1945 the ratio of defense R&D to procurement gradually increased from around 5 percent to a peak of over 50 percent, with cyclical variations during periods of conflict.)

The concentration of such a small number of firms, particularly in any given product area, leads to an environment of oligopolistic "rivalry" in which existing firms use their monopoly (or oligopoly) power to pay for large amounts of R&D in order to "win the next big contract" and to keep out potential new entrants: they "buy-in" so that they will get the follow-on production contract. This appears to work, since the same eight firms which had the giant share of the R&D dollars in 1977 also received a significant share of the defense production dollars spent that year. Additionally, the Defense Department allows firms to charge, as part of their allowable costs, an independent research and development (IR&D) account which is based on a percentage of sales, thus further amplifying the high level of industry concentration. Finally, because these large firms have significant lobbying power, both officially and unofficially, in the executive and legislative branches, they naturally have significant influence on the R&D decision-making process. The question is whether or not these factors are all positive in relation to the future defense posture of the nation.

In my opinion, the concentration in large firms has three very distinct impacts on the R&D decision process. First, these firms tend, as most large institutions do, to be risk minimizers, and thus tend not to push high-risk inventions – totally new ideas or applications, what I prefer to call quali-tative changes. Research is more likely to be done on in-creasing the speed of an airplane or tank than on developing some totally new device. The former is an incremental, or quantitative, change, while the latter would be an example of a qualitative change. Additionally, of course, this kind of R&D tends to fit well within the existing structure, to match the form and objectives of the current organizations (on both the industry and DOD sides) and to address the questions that these organizations are willing to ask. (More far-reaching questions normally pose a threat to these existing organizatons: for example, would pilots want the usefulness of airplanes questioned?)

R&D done by the large firms tends to be more of the in-novative type (development and exploitation of new ideas) than of the inventive type (the creation of new ideas). There are ample data from Blair(5) and Scherer(6) to docu-ment this innovative rather than inventive role of the large firms.(7) This comes in part from the institutional inertia of the large firms, and in part from their internal management decision process. Thus, the concentration within defense

R&D tends to emphasize low-risk, incremental change rather than the generation of really significant new departures. As will be seen below, there are many other structural considerations that tend to point in the same direction for defense R&D.

Consider next the strong emphasis on technology in the defense industry. Naturally, part of this comes from the military side wanting the best possible equipment - with the implication that cost is clearly less important than military performance in each weapon system. But it also comes from the management of a defense firm which in general is composed largely of engineers who have moved up through the organization, from designer to program manager to corporate officer. Their main emphasis is on the development and use of technology for improved performance with far less attention directed to the use of technology for reduced production costs or other considerations that dominate the commercial sector of U.S. industry - where, by contrast, the executives often come from finance, marketing, legal, or production departments.

Naturally, defense managers would tend to place considerable emphasis on R&D. Additionally, they would tend to place considerable emphasis on a heavy engineering content in their workforce and this is exactly what is found in the typical defense firm. Because the largest defense sector is the aerospace industry,(8) its constituents tend to be considered as "typical" defense firms; often between 30 and 50 percent of the total factory workforce are engineers and scientists. The question here is whether this large technical workforce is actually coming up with new ideas, or is simply applying the inventions of a few - from their firm or elsewhere.

First, from a vertical perspective, a very large share of the technical workforce of the major prime contractors eats up government R&D money on "systems work" at the expense of research and development on very critical component technology. From a horizontal cut, this technical workforce tends to consume an enormous amount of government R&D expenditure on full-scale developments of weapons systems, where they are doing largely routine work of converting feasibility-demonstrated systems into production drawings and the like, - which again uses up government R&D money that could be spent on far more creative activity, more "leading edge of technology" work. Thus these large percentages of engineers in each defense-industry facility tend to result in a very significant share of the work being done on the less creative aspects of R&D. By contrast, the French, for example, have very small percentages of engineers in their workforce, and operate with very small design teams, thus allocating a larger percentage of their military R&D funds for more creative activities.

An additional effect of this large number of engineers in a given plant is that considerable R&D money is spent on engineering work done on systems that are already in production, rather than on new systems. This practice accounts for the very large number of changes which take place on a typical defense item during its production phase. Frequently the presence of these engineers simply results in changes for the sake of change; for example, where an improvement in capability is only marginal, but the increase in cost is quite significant. In fact, there are many who argue that it is this heavy emphasis on engineering throughout the acquisition process and throughout the labor forces (on both sides of the military-industrial structure) that results in the so-called technological imperative being the largest single driving force in weapon system development; "because we can do it, we must do it" - regardless of the need or the cost!

A more recent, yet growing, consequence of the heavy engineering emphasis within the defense industry has been the tendency to emphasize technology in foreign military sales. This has been particularly true of firms who are less successful in the U.S. defense market. As a result, these firms have been willing to make significant "technology transfers" to foreign buyers to win orders and to keep their technical staffs employed. Examples of such "technology transfers" include design support, training and turn-key factories capable of manufacturing advanced-technology, and military equipment. This action in turn requires that the U.S. expend more R&D dollars in the area of the transferred technology in order to assure U.S. technological leadership; for example, if the transferred equipment contains countermeasures, then the U.S. needs to push forward more rapidly on counter-countermeasures. Thus, this action is self-rewarding for the defense firms in that field, but it does not necessarily make the best use of the government's defense R&D dollars.

Next, consider the effects of vertical integration in the defense industry - which traditionally has been heavily vertically integrated. An increasing amount of vertical integration has been taking place in the defense industry for a variety of reasons - for example, to maintain market share, to assure capability for bidding on new programs, to assure the availability of critical parts (in the presence of rapidly diminishing sources), and because of the financial problems at the lower tiers of the defense industry. Thus, subcontractors are being absorbed by prime contractors, and many of the prime contractors are building their own parts sources - for example, their integrated-circuits laboratories and their fabrication facilities for composite materials. The effect of this increasing vertical integration is to place even greater R&D emphasis on the system level of the dominant prime-contractor organizations and to eliminate the drive for technological innovation and invention at the lower levels - which, I believe, are the critical levels for future military advances.

There is a second category of "vertical integration" which exists in most sectors of the defense industry; namely, the fact that once a firm has won an R&D contract it is almost assured of being the sole-source producer for any subsequent production and logistics support equipment. This tie between R&D award and sole-source production is the key structural link in the defense industry, and is one which greatly influences the R&D decision-making process. Because of this kind of integration, there is an emphasis on R&D of items which have significant production potential in the near term - since the firm always has in mind the need to "keep its factories full." Thus, R&D is not a business unto itself, but is an entree into the production business. The result is a significant pressure to put all developments into production - although, in fact, many of these developments had been initiated as "alternatives" when the original intent was only to put one or the other into production.

In the Soviet Union, where R&D and production are separate, there are typically more alternatives developed relative to the units that go into production than in the U.S.. The tie of R&D to production in the U.S. means that each plant, or at least each firm, must have its own R&D capability and its own production capability. In view of the normally very small number of items in a defense-production program, this tends to result in quite inefficient production; yet, interestingly, this does not result in the R&D programs emphasizing production costs (for reasons that are discussed below).

Next, consider the barriers to entry which exist in the defense industry and which greatly discourage new firms from entering. These barriers are effectively of two types: first, those constructed to keep out the small firms, and second, those constructed to keep out large commercial firms. Looking at the first of these two types, we see at least ten barriers:

1. The government counts heavily, in its source selection, on prior technological experience to lend credibility to the claimed potential performance of the proposed design. Thus, one has to have had business in order to get business.

2. There is an extremely high cost to bidding. This frequently runs into the millions of dollars. Thus, only the large corporations can afford to compete.

3. The government will frequently issue invitations to bid only to "qualified sources," - those who have the existing plant and equipment to handle both the development and production programs.

4. The government will prohibit foreign competition on research-and-development contracts, due to security needs,

as well as promote legislation requiring domestic sources for defense R&D.

5. The government feels that the large companies, in the event of cost overruns or other financial problems, are more financially able to "weather the storm"; thus they have more confidence in going to them on high-risk programs. In reality, however, the financial risk is relatively small on these programs, since they are normally awarded on a cost-plus-fee basis.

6. Only the large corporations are in a position to support the extensive overhead required by the government in such areas as auditing, reporting, security, and data. The Defense Department "manages" these large development programs through literally thousands of reports submitted by the contractors.

7. The DOD prefers to reduce its own administrative load, to contract in "big chunks" rather than dispense a larger number of smaller contracts. This frequently rules out the small companies who might compete only on the smaller programs.

8. The large companies are usually the only ones who can afford the initial "buy-in" which frequently takes place during the early phases of a research-and-development competition. In fact, this ability to buy in is a principal way in which the large companies can keep out the small companies.

9. Since the contractual cycle is frequently a very uncertain one, with ups and downs due to the will of Congress and the annual budget cycle, the large companies are the only ones which can afford to carry their engineering personnel during the low periods in the cycle.

10. The DOD has usually emphasized "promised technical performance" as its primary criterion for selection of R&D products (and therefore of suppliers). By contrast, traditionally, the smaller firms and the more commercially oriented firms have been better at designing low-cost products - and these have not been particularly sought by the DOD.

The result of these barriers is to maintain the status of the large defense firms and to keep the small inventor-led firms from getting into the defense business. In my opinion, this practice discourages many new R&D ideas, particularly those leading to qualitative changes. Additionally, many other barriers keep even the large commercial firms from entering the defense business. These firms would, of course, tend to bring in the lower-cost philosophy of the commercial world. Here the barriers include:

- Low volume of work
- Specialized nature of the products - for example, military specifications

- Special reporting requirements, such as cost-accounting standards, and extensive paperwork costs, which raise the cost for competing on the commercial side
- Cyclical demand, rather than steady, long-term growth
- Security clearances
- Relatively low price-elasticity of demand

The last of these is particularly interesting. It implies that if you come up with a new idea for, say, a better or lower-cost airplane, you will simply be replacing the old one (in many cases this was your own) with very little likelihood of being able to create increased demand - since the numbers of airplanes to be procured are a function of the force structure, not a function of the cost of airplanes or of their performance. This relative insensitivity of military demand to lower-cost designs also discourages commercial firms from immediately turning to defense with any new products that they may have developed. Only much later is it likely that a defense-oriented firm might pick up the idea, and perhaps begin to apply it. By contrast, the Soviet Union tends to give first priority - on resources and skilled manpower - to its military area; so, most of their inventions originate there.

Lastly, in analyzing the structure of the defense industry, consider the distinct "dual economy" which exists between the prime contractors and the lower-tier subcontractors and parts suppliers. As noted above in the discussion of barriers faced by smaller firms in doing defense business, these lower levels must operate through the prime contractors. Thus, they tend to see an even larger cyclical variation in business - since, when business drops off, the prime contractors tend to do much more work "in-house." Additionally, the data clearly show that these lower tiers receive significantly less profit on their defense business, and do not have access to the government plants and equipment which the prime contractors do.

Defense prime contractors tend to have the highest R&D-to-capital-expenditure ratios of any sector in the U.S. economy;(9) for example, the aerospace industry has six to ten times the ratio of R&D-to-capital expenditures of the auto industry. By contrast, the small firms are required to make more significant capital investments and have lower profits, thus being unable to afford a large R&D expenditure. Similarly, the larger IR&D allowances of the prime contractors (based on a percentage of sales) discriminates against the smaller firms, as does the availability of government financing for the prime contractors, as opposed to the inability of the lower tiers to generate venture capital. Surprisingly, this "dual economy" is rarely recognized in establishing DOD policies - in terms of profit, source selection, or R&D policy; but it has a distinct impact on overall R&D decision making -

as, for example, when the preponderance of R&D dollars goes to the large prime contractors to do systems and full-scale development work, while the critical component technology work, often done by smaller firms, does not get proper emphasis.

THE IMPACT OF THE ACQUISITION PROCESS

The way in which the government does its business with the defense industry amplifies the above-described structural effects on military R&D decision making. The key characteristics of this process are:

- Public visibility and accountability of government decision makers and of defense firms
- Domination of full acquisition cycle by the winner of initial R&D competition
- Very long development time for weapon systems
- Highly cyclical and uncertain demand
- No industry-wide perspective - each project a separate decision

A key characteristic of most U.S. defense business (with the exception of that which is highly classified), and one which distinguishes the way in which government must do business in a democratic society such as in the U.S., is the very high level of public visibility and accountability required of the decision makers. The impact of this is that the decision makers feel they must minimize the risk associated with a research-and-development program. Thus, there is a tendency to give the business to large, well-established firms and, similarly, to select very conventional ideas for development. In my opinion, such results need not follow from the desirable requirements of visibility and accountability; rather, one can take high risks on R&D projects when there is a potentially high payoff. However, it should be explicitly stated by the decision makers that these are high-risk ventures (for example, contracts to relatively unproven firms, or funding for relatively unconventional ideas), and it may be necessary in some cases to develop "back-up" alternatives to these high-risk approaches. Nonetheless, it is these high-risk approaches which have traditionally resulted in the qualitative breakthroughs so necessary to maintain technological superiority over the long run.

Another impact of the requirement for public visibility and accountablility is that the primarily commercial firms tend to stay away from defense business, preferring not to provide the data required by, for example, the cost accounting

standards. Finally, there is the incredible amount of paperwork which goes along with the visibility and accountability
required in doing business with the government, and which
again prompts only the large, specialized, DOD-oriented firms
to do defense R&D. Here I believe that much of the paperwork is unnecessary. It provides "in process" visibility, but
simpler and cheaper ways can be realized to provide the
long-run visibility desired in a democratic society without
having so large a share of the overall R&D budget devoted to
paperwork. (On many programs this becomes a significant
percentage of the total dollars expended.)

     The second significant characteristic of the military R&D
decision-making process is that it normally begins with a competition for the initial R&D contract, and then the winner is
likely to continue on that project through the full acquisition
cycle - particularly into the large-dollar production programs
- on a sole-source basis. This situation greatly encourages
"buying-in" for the initial R&D program; that is, intentionally
bidding below cost in order to obtain the initial contract.
This form of cross-subsidization can only be done by large
firms, those which are realizing significant profits on their
production programs and are thus in a position to make their
initial R&D proposals extremely attractive to government
buyers. Taught by experience, the bidders can make highly
optimistic estimates on schedule and cost for the development
phase if they anticipate significant design changes coming
along during the development program (often introduced by
the technical people at the contractor's facility).

     Naturally, the effects of these changes are increased
costs for the overall development program, and stretched-out
schedules. To the contractor, this simply means a modification of his contract and the recovery of his initial "buy-in"
costs; to the outside world it looks like program "overrun"
and "slippage" - resulting in the reputation that military R&D
work has for mismanagement. It also naturally leads to a
great deal of industry emphasis on design changes to existing
products as a major R&D activity, to the detriment of new
ideas and new product development. Interestingly, the official attitude never assumes this to be the case. Thus, the
U.S. development approach begins with new programs, as
contrasted to the European or Soviet approaches which
acknowledge modifications as the desired methodology.

     Since the initial R&D program on which the competition is
held is usually for a relatively small dollar effort, and since
the bids themselves are made extremely attractive by the
bidders, the primary source selection is then based on technology and military performance. Thus, each of the bidders
is effectively <u>encouraged</u> to provide designs which have the
maximum possible military performance as their stated objectives - in contrast to the commercial world's design objectives

of maximum performance for a given unit production cost.

The approach of early competition followed by sole-source contracting through the remainder of the program provides no incentives for cost reductions, either in the R&D program or later in the production program. In fact, the incentives are in exactly the opposite direction: the contractor is encouraged to increase the development and production costs as much as possible, because this maximizes profits, and because in a sole-source environment there is no risk attached to doing so.

This lack of incentive for cost reduction should be compared with the commercial sector in which competition is maintained into production and therefore determines which technology is chosen to drive down the cost of systems - rather than solely to increase performance, as in the defense area. The failure to use technology for cost reduction is one of the distinguishing characteristics of defense R&D, and one which flows from the basic process under which defense R&D is performed. It results in the significant increase in unit cost of systems, year after year, in order to achieve increased performance in those systems - versus the reduced cost with increased performance that is seen in the commercial world. It results in U.S. defense systems being designed as expensive in comparison to those of other countries, even the Soviet Union.(10)

It must be emphasized that this DOD acquisition practice forms a mutually reinforcing relationship with the second form of vertically-integrated industrial structure described above; namely, each large firm having the capacity for both R&D and production. Thus the industry structure also prevents competition from naturally occurring at the beginning of production.

Finally, there is a belief, held mostly within the procurement community, that by mandating competition during the R&D phase, DOD officials are satisfying the legislative requirement to have competition on government procurements. Thus, there is a tendency to take new ideas submitted by "outsiders," or small firms, and to have those let out to competition. Through advertising and the process of Request for Proposals, the idea becomes widely disseminated, and the competition is usually won by a large firm utilizing cross-subsidization and a very "attractive" proposal - both in terms of the amount of money spent on the proposal effort as well as of the low cost of the proposed R&D activity. In this way new ideas from outside the existing defense industrial community are greatly discouraged by government procedures.

Another interesting characteristic of the defense R&D process is its increasingly long development cycle.(11) As an example, a 1976 Defense Science Board study of the fleet ballistic missile system indicated that, while Polaris A-1 went from concept to initial operational capability in less than five years, the Polaris A-3 took over six years, the Poseidon C-3 took nine years, and the Trident C-4 over eleven years. A most interesting point about this trend is the fact that it is exactly contrary to the direction of technological evolution, which, for example, makes a typical electronics production line obsolete in six months. Thus, not only does this long development cycle result in fielding obsolete equipment, it also results in an extremely inefficient utilization of R&D dollars, since, in this case, time is money. (The cost of the engineering staff, among others, will be applied to the program through its full duration).

Again, since the production dollars constitute the "carrot at the end of the stick," only large firms can afford to stay in for the ten years or more required for the development of a new weapon system. Naturally, this effect is recognized, but what is often neglected is that the same thing applies to the lower levels of the defense market. The small firm, doing the R&D work on critical components and subsystems, also has the ten-year wait, but with very little money coming in and often without even the assurance of receiving the production order. This further discourages R&D at the lower levels of the defense industry.

One effect of the U.S. annual budget process is the uncertainty associated with multi-year defense R&D programs. The way in which the business is done, particularly in regards to the strong tie between R&D and production, also results in a highly cyclical program for any one firm over a period of years. The combination of built-in cyclical behavior and uncertainty - often the result of executive and legislative whim, on either programs or dollars - results in an extreme emphasis on short-term R&D as well as a very inefficient use of the manpower and dollars allocated to these R&D programs. Clearly, much of this uncertainty and some of the cyclical nature of the business can be significantly reduced through changes in the way the DOD and the U.S. government do their business.

The last of the major characteristics of the defense acquisition process which significantly influences the R&D decision-making process is that associated with the lack of an industry-wide perspective in major program R&D decisions. Essentially, each major program is treated independently, and the choice of industrial source is made on the basis of the "optimum" choice for that particular program - unlike the industry-wide, longer-term perspective taken by almost every other country in the world. The result of this program-by-program perspective is that individual firms often go through a "boom or bust" cycle, reinforcing the short-term perspective in terms of R&D work, and this greatly discourages many creative scientists from going into defense research.

The argument often used against taking an industry-wide perspective is that the free market will take care of that. However it should be clear that the market in this case is a single buyer and usually just two or three suppliers. Thus, what is needed is for the government to recognize its role in this market and to introduce greater long-term industry stability, while maintaining strong competition between firms, so that technological advancement can be continued to be pushed and fully utilized - both for improved military performance and for reduced system costs.

IS INDUSTRIAL CREATIVITY REALLY ENCOURAGED?

Given the defense industrial structure and the acquisition process described above, one must ask whether or not they are successful in encouraging the creative R&D that is necessary for the continuation of the technological superiority of the U.S. military establishment. Overall, I would have to conclude that the results clearly indicate that the system works, since the U.S. has been able in the past to maintain a strong technological advantage over potential adversaries. However, in recent years the Soviets have been catching up. With their current level of R&D expenditures, which exceed the U.S. expenditures, with the clear demonstration of a narrowing of the technological gap, and with the technological assistance that they are receiving from the West, one can project forward and see the very real need for the U.S. to improve upon the efficiency of its R&D effort if it is to maintain a technological advantage in future years. Thus, it is appropriate to look at some of the areas in which U.S. industrial creativity is not being encouraged, and to make some specific suggestions for changes in these areas.

From the above discussion it is clear that I believe there is far too much R&D money going in the direction of supporting large engineering departments in each of the major defense firms. There is, in particular, excess spending on the "non-creative" aspects within such activities as full-scale development, systems engineering, drawings, reports, and data, rather than a commitment to critical feasibility demonstrations at the component, subsystem, and systems-integration levels.

Secondly, it should be clear from the above discussion that the DOD's preference for doing business only with the large, established firms discourages the sort of qualitative changes that would harmonize with the established corporate institutions, missions, or organizations. Thus, nontraditional firms, the small ones or the commercially-oriented ones, are discouraged from or kept out of defense business; yet they are more likely to be the firms where inventions and qualitative changes originate.

The area of corporate independent research and development (IR&D), in my opinion, is one of the very best potential sources of new research ideas, since the firm is in complete control of these dollars and uses them in much the same way that a commercial firm would use its research and development money; but Congress is constantly attacking this area's small percentage (5 percent) of the research and development money. Even within the DOD, many tend to react with disfavor to IR&D because the government does not fully control the project allocation of these funds. However, the small firms get little of the IR&D dollars, so they require added incentives and funding from the government in order to come up with new, creative ideas.

Finally, the government's lack of a long-term perspective on the industrial structure results in significant instability at the firm level. This causes an emphasis on short-term R&D, which tends to discourage outstanding scientists and engineers from going into the defense field.

In general, what is emphasized and is therefore done extremely well is incremental performance improvements to traditional military products; there is plenty of government support and industry motivation to achieve significant technological advances of this type. But the less traditional equipment areas, or those mission areas where new inventions or qualitative changes are desired, are much less likely to be stimulated through the current structure of the defense industry and the DOD process of acquiring R&D work on military equipment.

SUGGESTIONS FOR IMPROVING DEFENSE R&D

There are a number of specific actions which the Department of Defense can take (most of which require no legislative changes) that would significantly improve the use of defense R&D dollars in achieving DOD's objective of significant technological superiority of its forces for the minimum overall acquisition cost.

I believe that each of the recommendations listed below can bring about a significant improvement in the current situation. Some can be implemented relatively easily and rapidly; others will be more difficult, and therefore should be done over a longer period of time. Taken together, there is no question that these changes will result in major improvements in R&D decision making in the defense area.

- An in-house government <u>advocate</u> for nontraditional missions and nontraditional equipment research and development is needed. I would suggest that this begin in the Office of the Undersecretary for Research and Engineering, but also that there be equivalent organizations in each of the services.(12) Naturally, to be effective these groups must have an R&D budget (perhaps 5 percent of the overall R&D budget), they must be free of normal procedures and regulations, and be encouraged to deal with firms who are not traditional DOD suppliers.

- Much more integration of commercial and military R&D - at the plant level - should be encouraged, and a specific task force should be established to determine what steps are necessary in order to achieve this objective.

- There should be far more emphasis by the DOD on IR&D as an important tool for research and development. When selling this program to Congress it need not be done in an apologetic fashion. However, the DOD must ascertain that industry is using these funds in the way in which they were intended - for independent, long-term R&D, rather than as marketing funds or to absorb other R&D program overruns.

- There ought to be far more long-term stability as a primary consideration in R&D work in industry. One way of assuring this is through far greater use of multi-year funding. (Congress has frequently approved such funding, when it has been presented on a sound economic basis. I believe that more concrete steps can be taken in this direction.)

- There should be specific efforts made to place fewer dollars in the full-scale development of individual systems, and more dollars in the area of advanced development and feasibility demonstrations. This undoubtedly will require some changes in the way that R&D dollars are expended, and the way that full-scale development projects are managed; but I believe a significant effort can be made in this direction. One positive step would be the recognition that many advanced development projects are intended as <u>alternatives,</u> and that only a few among these will be selected for full-scale development. Other actions involve addressing the acquisition process itself - for example, by making better use of prototypes and thereby reducing full-scale development expenditures.

- There should be more R&D dollars set aside for component research and development so that this important area does not get ignored as a result of the structure of the defense industry and DOD procedures.

- There should be far more attention paid to the concept of <u>continuous</u> competition in given areas of technology.

In this way one could achieve greater R&D labor stability and also create significant incentives for technological advancement.

- Ways should be found to achieve far easier entry into the defense business for non-defense-oriented firms - both large and small - with <u>qualitatively</u> new ideas.

- The DOD must develop new incentives for productivity-enhancing and cost-reducing R&D. Currently, the incentives result in just the opposite effects.

- There must be changes made in the acquisition process that will result in significant shortening of the development cycle. This will get new technology into the field much faster, and with no likely increase in risk. The shorter time period will also result in far lower cost for the full-scale development of systems, since, in many cases, time spent and dollars spent are directly proportional. This shortening of the overall development cycle can be achieved partly by making decisions in parallel with equipment development, rather than having long, six- to nine-month periods in which all development stops while the decision-making process reviews the alternatives for the next step.

- The DOD should make a greater effort to separate R&D and production on the industrial side, so that R&D can become a credible business unto itself, and so that production can become more efficient through specialization.

- More awards of <u>initial</u> R&D contracts should be done on a sole-source basis. Thus unsolicited proposals would be encouraged for new ideas, and the individual or firm submitting them would have confidence that he would be able to begin the effort without competing (for his idea) with many of the large firms. This action, combined with more competition in the later phases of the acquisition process, would result in far more of the total DOD dollars being awarded on the basis of competition than is currently the case. Also, it would result in the stimulation and encouragement of many new ideas from defense firms and new entrants.

- There must be a plan, or acquisition strategy, developed that will maintain the U.S. technological-leadership position while achieving allied forces standardization and optimum use of the combined NATO resources. For example, it could be required that in any area in which the U.S. agreed to transfer technology, or agreed to European development, it would immediately begin initial research on the next generation of technology in that area.

- There should be far more conscious R&D emphasis on the use of technology for cost reduction, rather than regarding this simply as a possible fall-out, as is primarily the case today.

These are obviously just a few of the possible changes
that could be made to improve the way in which defense R&D
decision making takes place. In the past the DOD has done a
good job in its R&D decision making - as demonstrated by
proven U.S. military technological superiority. However, in
the rapidly changing geopolitical and technological era of the
1980s, it will be necessary for the DOD to change its way of
doing business and change its supporting industrial structure
to keep pace with external changes and maintain its technological superiority into the twenty-first century.

NOTES

(1) Here I am using the traditional industrial-organization
     economist's model; that is, structure affects conduct,
     which affects performance. See F.M. Scherer, Industrial
     Market Structure and Economic Performance (Chicago:
     Rand McNally, 1970). Additionally, I am using some of
     my own prior work on the influence of "the way in which
     the government does its business" on the structure (and
     therefore the conduct and performance) of the defense
     industry. See J.S. Gansler, "Let's Change the Way the
     Pentagon Does Business," Harvard Business Review,
     May-June 1977; and J.S. Gansler, The Defense Industry
     (MIT Press, late 1980).
(2) Rockwell, General Electric, General Dynamics,
     McDonnell-Douglas, Boeing, Lockheed, Hughes, and
     Raytheon.
(3) U.S. Department of Defense, 500 Contractors: Con-
     tractors receiving the largest dollar volume of military
     prime contract awards for RDT&E (FY 77).
(4) Scherer, Industrial Market Structure, p. 373.
(5) J. M. Blair, Economic Concentration: Structure, Be-
     havior, and Public Policy (New York: Harcourt Brace
     Jovanovich, Inc., 1975), p. 204.
(6) Scherer, Industrial Market Structure, p. 356.
(7) To be fair, there are many who argue this point, based
     upon the need for large capital investments in today's
     high technology world. Also, I do not mean to imply
     that large firms are excluded from making inventions;
     rather, I am discussing the historical, and likely future,
     trends.
(8) In 1975 the aerospace industry received 45 percent of
     the $9.5 billion of defense R&D dollars.
(9) H. R. Clauser, "News and Views of the Current Re-
     search Management Scene," Perspectives (Washington
     D.C.: Industrial College of Armed Forces), p.1.

(10)   A study done by an intelligence agency, and released
       in an unclassified form in 1976, showed a comparison
       between comparable Soviet jet engines and U.S. jet en-
       gines, under the assumption that both were to be built
       with U.S. materials and labor in the same U.S. plant.
       It found that the Soviet engine would actually cost be-
       tween one-third and one-half of the cost of the com-
       parable-performance U.S. engine.   It is believed that a
       significant part of this difference is accounted for by
       the fact that the Soviets design for "producibility" while
       the U.S. designs almost exclusively for maximum per-
       formance - and thus does not simultaneously achieve
       low-cost production.
(11)   Interestingly, this same combination of increased devel-
       opment time and increased development costs have been
       seen in other fields - as the government becomes more
       involved.   For example, in 1960 it took about two and
       one-half years and $1.5 million to bring a new drug to
       the marketplace; in 1978 it took up to ten years and
       around $15 million, including getting approval of the
       Food and Drug Administration (Fortune, January 30,
       1978, p. 121).
(12)   DARPA, being technology oriented and outside of the
       service organizations, has a different role than the one
       described here.

III

The Genesis of
New Weapons

5 Conception of New Defense Systems and the Role of Government R & D Centers

Alexander Kossiakoff

For the past two and one-half decades the U.S. has devoted substantial resources to the development and acquisition of new, technologically advanced military weapons and related systems. The magnitude and importance of this effort, and criticism of many of its products, has led the executive and legislative branches of the government to devote a great deal of attention to enhancing the effectiveness of its management. Emphasis has focused on the issues concerned with the acquisition of what are referred to as "major systems" - military systems requiring large expenditures over a period of many years. The decisions of greatest moment are those relating to how such programs are conceived, defined, and selected for full-scale development and production.

This chapter addresses two related aspects of the military R&D decision process. The primary aspect is an analysis of the conceptual phases of the development of major defense systems in terms of their constituent steps and decision points. The secondary one is the special role played by government-supported R&D centers during the establishment of mission needs and during the formulation and evaluation of concepts designed to meet such needs. There will be only brief reference to R&D for technology-base development or to the later phases of system development, production, and operation, except as they provide an essential basis of knowledge for the conceptual phase. The important role of industrial contractors during the formative phases of system acquisition will be noted, but discussion of it will be limited mainly to issues of acquisition strategy and to its interaction with that of the R&D centers.

To provide a frame of reference for discussing the conception of new defense systems, the initial sections of this chapter will define three different aspects of system acquisition: institutional, functional, and procedural.

The first section deals with the institutional aspect, and categorizes the different types of organizations engaged in the defense R&D effort, with particular reference to those which are wholly dedicated to working for the government. The latter grouping includes the in-house R&D centers of the military services, government-sponsored university laboratories, and independent, not-for-profit organizations established to support certain defense missions. All of these organizations are in a manner of speaking "in-house," insofar as they are under the direct sponsorship of the government and dedicated to supporting its activities. The term Defense R&D Centers will be used for this grouping.

The second section treats the process of originating and implementing a military weapon system, resolving it into four functional elements, and relating each to the military and supporting organizations which are its principal contributors. These elements are: (1) assessment of operational effectiveness and need, (2) advancement of knowledge and technology, (3) production of new or improved operational equipment, and (4) definition of solutions to operational needs - the last serving the central function of coupling the first three together.

The third section identifies the policies and procedures which have been developed to govern the decision processes in major system acquisition, and some of their consequences. It describes the disaggregation of the acquisition process into discrete phases, punctuated by top-level decisions at specific milestones, and notes the cyclical nature of the process as it proceeds from the initial to succeeding generations of a major defense system.

The next two sections of the chapter discuss the essential elements of the conceptual phases of the development of defense systems, and analyze how they contribute to the formulation of system concepts to meet operational needs and to the selection of those meriting development. These are the most critical phases in the total acquisition process, and ones to which defense R&D centers make unique contributions.

The final section briefly summarizes the phases of defense system development, production, and operation, and the contribution to these activities by R&D centers. First-hand experience in the problems of system integration, producibility, reliability, and the operational environment, provides an invaluable feedback into the formulation of mission needs and concepts for follow-on systems.

INSTITUTIONAL ASPECTS OF MILITARY
RESEARCH AND DEVELOPMENT

Conception, development, and production of defense systems
are supported by a broad spectrum of government and private
organizations. This diversity is an intrinsic source of
strength, and affords the potential to apply the best available
resources to each important defense program.   While any
means of classification is necessarily an oversimplification,
Figure 5.1 categorizes organizations in terms of their relation
to the government, with illustrative examples in each category. In the first category are organizational units of the
government itself; in this instance, in-house laboratory
centers.   At the extreme right are independent industrial
companies which carry out military R&D but whose main orientation is commercial. In between are nonprofit and profit-
making organizations whose primary effort is in support of
military R&D.   One of the points illustrated in Figure 5.1 is
that the association of the government and the private sector
in support of military R&D takes on many forms which together constitute a versatile base for the defense effort.

Defense R&D Centers

The first three categories in Figure 5.1 fall into the general
classification of defense R&D centers, being wholly sponsored
by the government. In-house R&D centers, operated by each
of the armed services to provide essential support to system
acquisition functions, constitute by far the largest number of
organizations belonging to this grouping. Of these, the Navy
laboratory structure is the largest, principally owing to the
Navy's missions in ocean warfare, which require special facilities and involve equipment for which no industrial base
exists. By contrast, the Air Force, with major missions in
aircraft and electronics, has the fewest large in-house centers, relying more on contracts with industry. Boyd gives
an illuminating overview of the responsibilities and functions
of the Navy R&D centers, and discusses their roles in government decision making and in helping it function as a
"smart buyer."(1) All of the service R&D centers devote a
major portion of their effort to the technology base in special
areas of primary military application.
     University-sponsored R&D centers fall into two catego-
ries - laboratories and systems-analysis organizations. Most
of the former are the direct outgrowth of a pattern established during World War II. The two largest university
laboratories are The Johns Hopkins University Applied
Physics Laboratory, first established in 1942, and the MIT

AUSPICES	GOVERNMENT	PRIVATE			
DEDICATION	GOVERNMENT OWNED	GOVERNMENT SPONSORED NON-PROFIT		GOVERNMENT DEDICATED INDUSTRY	INDEPENDENT INDUSTRY
ORGANIZATION TYPE	IN-HOUSE LABORATORY	UNIVERSITY LABORATORY	INDEPENDENT NON-PROFIT	GOV'T OWNED COMPANY OPERATED	DEFENSE INDUSTRY	COMMERCIAL INDUSTRY
EXAMPLES	NAVAL WEAPONS CENTER	MIT LINCOLN LABORATORY	MITRE CORPORATION	GENERAL DYNAMICS POMONA DIV.	TRW DEFENSE SPACE SYSTEMS GROUP	TEXAS INSTRUMENTS
	ROME AIR DEVELOPMENT CENTER	JHU/APPLIED PHYSICS LABORATORY	DRAPER LABORATORY	ALLEGANY BALLISTICS LAB. (HERCULES)	LOCKHEED MISSILES & SPACE CO.	GENERAL MOTORS CORP.
	HARRY DIAMOND LABORATORY	LOS ALAMOS NATIONAL LABORATORY	RAND PROJECT AF	OAK RIDGE NATIONAL LABORATORY (UNION CARBIDE)	RAYTHEON MISSILE SYSTEMS DIVISION	A.D. LITTLE INC.

Fig. 5.1. Government-related Military R&D organizations

Lincoln Laboratory, established in 1950 on the foundation built by the wartime Radiation Laboratory. The latter category includes the Institute for Defense Analyses (IDA) which supports the Office of the Secretary of Defense, and the Center for Naval Analyses (CNA) operated by the University of Rochester. The systems analysis organizations contribute directly to decision-making processes at the level of mission and major systems, both to the formulation of needs and to the evaluation of current capabilities.

The three principal independent nonprofit corporations dedicated to defense R&D are the Rand Corporation (Project Air Force), the Aerospace Corporation and the MITRE Corporation, all operating under Air Force sponsorship. The focus of effort is systems analysis in the case of Rand, and systems engineering and systems integration in the case of Aerospace and MITRE. Among other nonprofit defense R&D centers, several were originally under university sponsorship, an example being Draper Laboratory, which was formerly part of MIT.

In an interesting paper, Norman Waks, chief management scientist of the MITRE Corporation, has described the formation of MITRE and how it has endeavored to serve a "bridge-like" role between the scientific community, the government, and industry.[2] This analogy has general validity in relating the roles of independent defense R&D centers to government and industry in large-scale military R&D programs.

There is abundant literature on the question of how the government should support its R&D operations by use of in-house and other dedicated R&D centers.[3] For example, the Federal Contract Research Centers (FCRCs), a somewhat artificially selected group of university-sponsored and independent nonprofit organizations dedicated to defense R&D, have been studied most recently by the Duffy Committee under the auspices of the Defense Science Board. Most of the literature deals with the institutional relationships of these organizations to the government and to industry - and in the case of the latter, to their competitive aspects, potential or real.

In connection with the decision-making process and sources of new military weapons, functional relationships are of greater interest, including the complementarity and mutual support between defense R&D centers and defense industry.

Role of Industry in Defense R&D

As in the case of the defense R&D centers, the types of industrial organizations engaged in defense R&D take on many forms. One special form is that of the government-owned company-operated (GOCO) organizations, in which the government has chosen to own specialized production, engineering, and research facilities, and to contract with private industry to operate them. Such organizations are primarily concerned with engineering and manufacture of military devices in technology areas where no commerical base exists, or where the government desires to insure adequate reserve mobilization facilities.

The term "defense industry" is generally applied to companies which have chosen to dedicate essentially all their efforts to the development of defense products, or have established divisions devoted to this purpose. These are organizations listed in the "dedicated industry" column of Figure 5.1; although they compete in the defense market for new products, many of their facilities are government owned. Many of these companies have been able to maintain long-term continuity in their defense activities, especially when involved in evolutionary weapon system programs.

There is, of course, no sharp boundary between such organizations and "independent" industry that is largely in the commercial market. However, there tends to be a difference between the role which so-called defense industry plays and that which "independent industry" plays, especially in the area of competition for defense products. While the examples cited in Figure 5.1 are large companies, an important and increasing role in defense R&D is played by smaller organizations.

The focus of this paper is on the early conceptual stages of the development of major military systems, and predominantly on the role of the defense R&D centers in these stages. Even while emphasizing these particular institutions, it would be misleading not to point out that the defense industries have an important role not only in the production of the system but in the initial conceptual development. Industrial groups perform a substantial amount of military R&D. Much of this is on specific development projects; that is, in the phases following the formulation of concepts. However, industry also contributes to the development of new ideas and new systems concepts. This is naturally the case in the development of proposed upgraded systems that are a follow-on to items in production by a given company. Industry also accomplishes a good deal of research on new concepts, much of it utilizing government funding under the independent research and development (IR&D) support program of the Defense Department. It is therefore important, as one turns to the broader aspects of systems acquisitions, to keep in mind the significant role of the defense industry and the continuing interactions which occur between R&D centers, industry, and the military services.

FUNCTIONAL ELEMENTS OF DEFENSE
SYSTEMS ACQUISITION

As a background for discussing the system acquisition
process, it is illuminating to resolve the activities and objectives constituting this process into four functional elements, as shown in Figure 5.2.

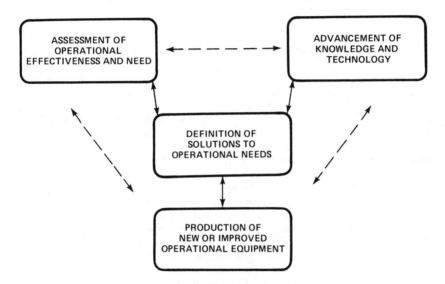

Fig. 5.2.   Components of Defense system acquisition.

In the upper left block of the diagram is the task of
assessing a military mission area in terms of the vulnerability
and effectiveness of available resources, and determining
whether a need exists for new or improved operational capabilities.   This task involves activities closely coupled to
military operations, including threat assessment, operations
analysis, and operational test and performance assessment.
In the upper right block is the task of building a foundation of relevant knowledge and a technology base not necessarily directed toward a specific operational capability, but
on which system development can draw.   The activities involved are research and the development of new techniques
and devices, but not their production.   In the bottom block
is the task of producing the operational equipment, new or
upgraded, which can best fill operational needs.   It includes
development and engineering needed to support this objective.

In the center of the diagram, connected interactively to each of the corners, is the task of combining an understanding of the operational need, of the available technology, and of the industrial engineering and production potential to synthesize system requirements which are operationally adequate, technically achievable, and obtainable from the existing industrial base. This task includes activities referred to as "general systems engineering," "systems architecture," and/or "systems integration." In this chapter the term "general systems engineering" will be used to encompass these activities.

Organizational Roles in System Acquisition

The functions displayed in Figure 5.2 obviously depend on broad and intimate understanding of operational problems, access to intelligence information and long-term association with a military mission area. For the function of operations analysis, the Air Force and Navy depend mainly on Rand and CNA, while the Army depends on several in-house analysis groups and some contractors. The Institute for Defense Analysis is an important contributor to the support of DOD-wide systems analysis. Operational tests and assessment of the results are performed mainly by military personnel or in-house centers. In summary, the "assessment" element is uniquely the province of the government, supported by wholly dedicated organizations. This is not to say that support is not provided by independent organizations, but that is largely on a special case basis.

The production of operational equipment is equally clearly the province of industry. Defense products, large and small, constitute a substantial fraction of the output of private industry, and, as stated previously, represent virtually the total output of defense-dedicated industrial organizations. Into this task goes the development, engineering, testing, and other activities necessary to carry a requirement into a producible device or system. In certain areas where there is no commercial market or where special facilities are required, the government produces its own material, such as certain types of ammunition and mines. However, these government production activities represent only a minute fraction of the total.

In contrast to the above, the element in Figure 5.2 entitled "Advancement of Knowledge and Technology" is not the exclusive domain of any organizational sector. Direct support of this activity by the Department of Defense is distributed among universities, in-house R&D centers, and industrial organizations. IR&D funds spent by industry as well as commercial R&D should also be considered to contribute significantly to the advancement of the technology base.

The central element of Figure 5.2 is "Definition of Solutions to Operational Needs," and in this area the defense R&D centers play a key role. Rather than being the exclusive preserve of a given type of organization, however, this task is one in which military personnel, defense R&D centers, and industry must work closely together. The defense R&D centers play the "bridge" role, integrating the diverse ingredients necessary to formulate solutions appropriate to the need. To carry out this function requires competence and intimate knowledge of the three elements which must interact. Equally important is that the "bridging" organization must be highly adaptive, complementing rather than competing with capabilities of industry, as well as serving the special needs of the government organizations for program management.

The defense R&D centers bring to this central function special qualifications stemming from their first hand experience in the test, evaluation, and support of operational systems, and in their orientation toward problem solving rather than to a product line. The former is important in recognizing and appraising the real need for new or improved mission capabilities, as well as the practicality and utility of a potential technical concept. The latter provides a favorable condition for objectivity, combined with experience and knowledge.

POLICIES GOVERNING MAJOR SYSTEMS ACQUISITION

The Department of Defense has devoted great effort to develop a well-defined and disciplined decision process in the acquisition of major systems. Especially since McNamara and Hitch brought the concept of "systems analysis" to the management of defense programs, there has been continous growth in the degree of control which the Department of Defense has sought to exercise over the initiation and management of the acquisition of major systems. Recently the Office of Management and Budget entered the arena, promulgating government-wide policies for the management of procurement. The Congress has also greatly increased its scrutiny of program appropriations, often down to a detailed level, and has established a substantial staff to support this activity.

As a result, a number of policy-level program-management techniques have been introduced, many of them triggered by perceived failures of a particular program, but made to apply to all. These include such approaches as "contract definition," "total package procurement," "fly before buy," and "design to cost." Almost all of these have been based on good ideas, but they often have suffered from an elaboration of interpretative regulations and indiscriminate application.

Some of these techniques are in use today, and the principles of others have been incorporated in present policies. Anyone interested in understanding the military R&D decision process must be familiar with these policies and the accompanying procedures and terminology. Since these matters are in a continual state of evolution, even those who have generally followed the acquisition process may not be aware of the most recent procedures and of the changes pending.

Government Policy Directives

The policies governing the development of major systems are embodied in several directives issued by the Office of Management and Budget and by the Office of the Secretary of Defense. The three most important and relevant ones are OMB Circular A-109, and DOD Directives 5000.1 and 5000.2.

OMB Circular A-109 establishes policies to be followed by all executive branch agencies in the acquisition of major systems. It directs agencies to express needs and objectives in mission-oriented instead of hardware-oriented terms, to formalize the "front-end" of the process, to develop alternative concepts in a competitive environment, to give early consideration to priorities, risks, and affordability, to rely on private industry, and to tailor acquisition strategies to individual programs. Implementation by DOD of the requirements of A-109 has been accomplished by incorporating its provisions in DOD Directives 5000.1 and 5000.2.

Directive 5000.1 divides the process of major systems acquisition into phases separated by decision milestones, and establishes policy guidance for program management in each phase. Directive 5000.2 supplements 5000.1 and defines the composition and functions of the advisory councils (DSARCs), and the decision documents mission element need statement (MENS) and decision coordination paper (DCP).

Impact on Acquisition Management

In general, the policies and procedures of A-109 and the more detailed DOD directives designed to ensure an orderly and disciplined decision process, are fairly well structured to minimize the prosecution of ill-founded programs, gross overcommitments, and inadequate evaluation of the end product. The price for these benefits, however, has thus far proved great in terms of extending the time of acquisition and restricting freedom to manage the program effectively to respond to changing needs. Most importantly, they have placed reliance on rules and regulations rather than on placing the

best people in leadership positions, supporting them with resources, and allowing them flexibility to get the job done effectively.

A summer study carried out by the Defense Science
Board in 1977 recommended a number of specific changes to
the DOD directives designed to shorten acquisition time and
increase flexibility. These are in part incorporated in the
most recent revisions to DOD directives now under review,
but it remains to be seen whether these changes will have the
intended impact.

In particular, the objective of shortening the acquisition
time is extremely important to achieve. This will be most
difficult because in the present approach all factors combine
to minimize risk of failure. There is no comparable mechanism
to weigh the risk to the nation of incurring a delay in the
acquisition of a needed military capability. Unfortunately,
this tends to be an intangible judgment, and hence is not
entered into the present procedures. Until it is explicitly
treated, stated objectives to shorten acquisition time are not
likely to have much effect except to result in the failure to
initiate promising but high-risk (and hence conceivably long-
term) programs.

Structure of the Acquisition Process

Figure 5.3 depicts the formal phases of the development and
use of major defense systems, and shows where the major
decisions are made during the phases which precede production. The upper portion of the figure shows relative costs
for each of the program phases in a representative major
program. It is noteworthy that operational costs for the life
of the system can constitute a large investment, often quite
comparable to the acquisition costs.

In many instances, a mission need may be effectively
satisfied by upgrading a current system rather than developing a new one. As shown by the dotted line, costs for
upgrading (modernizing) are generally far less than for new
development, as is the time for accomplishment. These may
or may not be offset by the shorter useful life, possibly
higher operating cost, and lesser capability of the upgraded
system.

Figure 5.4 is another representation of the major system
acquisition process. This chart shows the same steps as Figure 5.3, but in the form of a circle in which the last phase
of the acquisition process is joined to the initial phase. This
corresponds to the fact that during the time between program
initiation and system deployment and operation, mission analysis may show that new needs have arisen which warrant initiation of a second cycle of system development. In evolu-

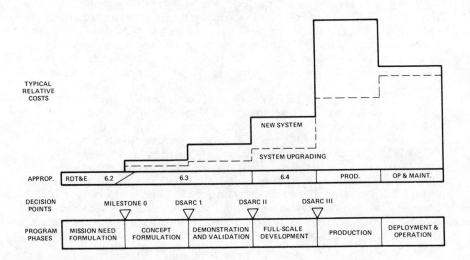

Fig. 5.3. Phases in life of major defense systems.

tionary programs, which are common for large-scale systems,
the second cycle may be limited to replacement of one or more
major subsystems within the same overall system framework.
    The remainder of this chapter will concentrate on the
decisions involved in the three blocks at the top of the circle
in Figure 5.4 (mission analysis, evaluation and formulation of
mission needs, and concept formulation). The decisions made
or not made during this period have an impact on the remainder of the program which is far greater than the magnitude of
the effort involved might imply.

MISSION ELEMENT NEED FORMULATION

The first official decision point of a new acquisition cycle for
major military system is labeled "Milestone Zero." To help insure that new programs respond to real military need, the
current DOD directives require the development and approval
of a formal mission element needs statement (MENS) prior to
the formal initiation of a new R&D program. As seen in Figure 5.4, there are two major components to the development
of a MENS: mission analysis, and evaluation and reconciliation
of needs. Figure 5.5 is an attempt to represent in diagram-
matic form the various elements involved in these two
functions.

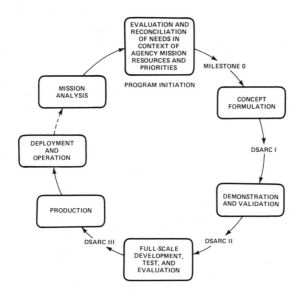

Fig. 5.4.   Major system acquisition cycle.

Mission Analysis

At the extreme left of the flow diagram in Figure 5.5 are the
main inputs to the formulation of an operational requirement
to fulfill a mission need.   One of these involves the postula-
tion of a projected threat or mission goal based on intelligence
estimates and technological forecasts.   This step in itself involves important judgments,   and involves a decision on
whether to emphasize near-term capabilities, at the risk of
early obsolescence, or longer-range goals with their greater
uncertainties.
     Given a well-defined threat model or goal, the degree of
difficulty in assessing the performance of current systems
depends on the complexity of the threat scenarios, the complexity of the system, and quantitative knowledge regarding
the effects of the operational environment.   To illustrate, for
the case of defending a Navy task force against a concerted
attack by air and submarine launched missiles, a valid assessment is a formidable undertaking.   Simplifying the com-
putation by leaving out important elements, such as the effects of countermeasures, can render the results meaningless.
     The other input to the decision process is the assess-
ment of the reliability, availability, and maintainability - or in
short, the "readiness" - of current assets.   This analysis
requires quantitative inputs from field operations conducted
under conditions simulating combat as closely as possible.

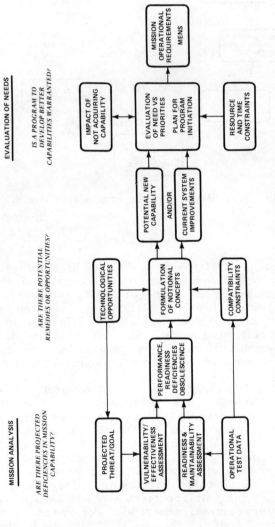

Fig. 5.5. Mission element need formulation.

74

These inputs lead to the definition of performance deficiencies or cost-saving opportunities, as, for example, the possibility of using advanced electronics technology to reduce manning costs.

Evaluation and Reconciliation of Needs

The above results in themselves do not lead to a conclusion that a program should be initiated. A necessary intermediate step is to determine that there is at least one credible approach which is realistic and compatible with the limitations imposed by the platform or other operational constraints, and which is likely to realize the desired objectives. This step is shown in the box marked "Formulation of Notional Concepts."

The term "notional concepts" does not connote system designs, but refers to the process of relating the perceived mission needs to conceivable means for fulfilling them by taking advantage of technological opportunities which have occured since the current systems were first defined - a period often of more than a decade. This process should consider both the possibility of meeting the objectives by improving an existing system, as well as that of developing an entirely new system. The result should be a conclusion as to whether one or both of the above approaches merits evaluation as a potential mission need.

In the final step of deciding whether or not to recommend a new program start, consideration of relative priorities must be brought in because of the inevitable competition for funds and resources. An important element in assigning priority should be to weigh the impact of not acquiring the capability in terms of the risk that current forces may be unable to perform the necessary mission. As stated previously, this factor is difficult to assess, but its formal introduction into the decision process should help assure that the risks of inaction are recognized and weighed. Thus it represents a definite step toward offsetting imbalances which exist today in the forces governing the R&D process.

The purpose of preparing a formal needs document for approval prior to initiating an active program is to ensure that adequate preliminary thinking has been done to establish a bona fide need, and that the need is defined in terms sufficiently specific to include all relevant constraints, but also sufficiently broad so as not to constrain the solution from considering a range of alternatives. Milestone 0 is the decision point at which the formal approval is handed down.

One of the difficulties in executing this important initial part of the system acquisition process is that most military agencies are not organized or staffed to accomplish the necessary assessment and evaluation, and thus far have had difficulty in getting MENS formulated and approved. There is a "chicken-and-egg" problem arising from the fact that a program manager cannot be appointed before a program is approved, while at the same time the scope and complexity of the task is such as to require a competent leader with authority to assemble and organize the resources needed to carry out all of its requirements properly.

The formulation of military needs is peculiarly a task for the government itself, supported by agencies directly responsible to it and with the necessary knowledge and point of view to provide the information needed to make the decisions. This is where mission-oriented, defense R&D centers can and do play a major supporting role, although the services also utilize studies performed by industrial contractors. In their respective mission areas, the R&D centers have a firsthand knowledge of capabilities and limitations of current systems, which puts them in a position to articulate operational needs and to recognize cost-saving opportunities in operation and maintenance. The system orientation of these organizations qualifies them to judge whether or not it is likely that the perceived need can in fact be satisfied within the existing state of the art and the operational constraints.

CONCEPT FORMULATION

The first formal phase of a major system acquisition process - that is, after Milestone 0 is passed - is referred to as the "concept formulation" or "program initiation" phase. It is in many respects the most critical with regard to program decisions and their potential impact on the ensuing program. Except where the program represents a major upgrading of a current system, this phase is a transitional process in which the entire program organization must take shape, along with the technical approach to meeting the mission need. It involves designating a program manager and establishment of a supporting staff to make and implement the difficult decisions required in initiating a new program. One of these decisions is to select the contracting strategy for the overall system development. These tasks must be carried out despite the fact that, except in rare instances, funding for new programs is low until they become well established in the budget cycle. In order to define more clearly the main elements and decision processes of this phase of the program, Figure 5.6 represents them as a functional flow diagram. The process is not a simple one, but consists of two basically distinct portions, requirements validation and concept definition, whose management is usually quite different.

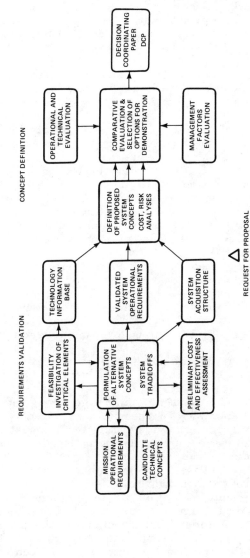

Fig. 5.6. Concept formulation process.

Requirements Validation

The requirements validation part of the concept-formulation phase revolves around the preliminary formulation and assessment of alternative concepts, taking the broadest possible view of the stated mission's operational requirements. The functions indicated include experimental investigations of those critical design elements which are not susceptible to analytical evaluation, preliminary cost assessment to indicate whether proposed concepts are affordable within available resources, and effectiveness assessment of the proposed systems.

The primary output of this effort is a revised operational requirement, in which a realistic balance has been struck among performance, cost, and schedule objectives. This is termed a "validated system operational requirement" in the figure, but it is still meant to be mission oriented rather than hardware oriented, specifying <u>what</u> the government wants rather than <u>how</u> it should be designed.

A second output is the creation of technological information relevant to the system concepts to be selected for demonstration. The magnitude of effort required to provide an adequate technology base is a direct function of the degree to which the desired new capability departs from proven technology, and the state of knowledge concerning the operational environment. In the case of straightforward extensions to existing technology, most of the answers might be obtainable by analysis or simulation. Conversely, for major technological innovations (for example, high-energy lasers), or for systems operating in very complex environments (for example, homing torpedoes), the extent of experimental investigations needed to establish valid design parameters might require several years of effort.

A third output of the requirements-validation process is the decision of how to configure the system and structure the acquisition process with respect to the degree of contractor responsibility for development and engineering of the total system and its elements. To the maximum extent practicable, the system should be subdivided into the subsystems corresponding to existing expertise in industrial engineering and production, product lines, and facilities. This is important not only to obtain satisfactory performance but to guarantee that meaningful competition will be possible.

The requirements-validation process is one which should utilize the combined forces of defense R&D centers and industrial contractors under the direction of the program management organization. It is important that during this period maximum information is shared between R&D centers, which are expert in the operational and technical problems within the mission area, and contractors interested in competing for

system or subsystem development. However, such communication for all practical purposes is impossible if formal
industrial competition is introduced prematurely and judged,
to a significant degree, on the basis of proprietary ideas and
information possessed by potential competitors; the inevitable
result is an incomplete and deficient requirement definition.
Such will not be the case if formal competition between firms
is based on the completed and validated requirement. The
participation of potential contractors in the requirements-
validation process can be accomplished through informal
contracting procedures, using funded studies and experiments
as well as IR&D agreements. This method of operation, which
is quite common, permits contractors to contribute ideas, to
learn the problems, to apply their expertise in the conduct of
feasibility investigations of critical subsystems, and to qualify
as bidders. It also permits defense R&D centers to contribute ideas freely, and carry out feasibility investigations as
appropriate without engaging in direct competition with industrial contractors. The government helps to insure that it
is not only a "smart buyer" but also that it will be able to
depend on the availability of "smart bidders," while the
defense R&D centers further contribute to the decision process by evaluating trade-off analyses of requirements which
stress technical risk and system cost.

System Acquisition Architecture

In most directives it is implied that the total system will be
developed by a single prime contractor, who will do the overall systems engineering and subcontract such subsystems as
may be product lines or other companies. This presupposes
that the system can be defined in isolation from other related
systems, and that several contractors have adequate capability to develop it as an integrated package. Under these conditions, the optimum strategy is to use a competitively selected, prime system contractor. However, in major complex
systems the above approach is seldom practicable, because
contractors with the breadth of expertise necessary to carry
out the systems engineering and development of the entire
system are simply not available. This is the case, for example, for shipboard or submarine combat systems, which
themselves consist of major elements such as surveillance
systems, fire control systems, launching systems, and missiles, all integrated into a tactical data system. Each of
these is itself a complex system involving one or more industrial product lines. In such cases, alternative acquisition
strategies are indicated.
     If prime contractors are available who, while not capable
of assuming total systems engineering responsibility, have

demonstrated the capability of managing the integration of
comparable systems once the subsystems have been defined
and developed, the preferred strategy is either to contract
separately for selected subsystems requiring development, or
to stipulate their acquisition through directed subcontracts.
This style of contracting is common in acquiring airborne
systems, in which the airframe contractor generally serves as
the prime, while engines and complex avionics systems may be
developed under separate contracts. Finally, if no appropriate system prime contractor is available, a separate contractor
may be utilized for the function of system integration and
testing, or the government may serve in that capacity and
assemble a team of subsystem contractors. This is the mode
of contract management in both the Air Force and Navy
strategic system programs.

It is obvious that this strategy must be defined as early
in the program as possible in order to establish the ground
rules for industry participation in each stage of the acquisition process. Otherwise, contractors who have no chance to
be selected may expend considerable effort to qualify for
program participation. But the decision cannot be made
before the requirements are defined to the point where the
proper system architecture becomes evident; hence the
requirements-validation phase is the appropriate time to formulate this decision.

Concept Definition

The final stage of the concept-formulation process develops
the concept to the place where approval can be sought to
proceed to validation and demonstration of selected options,
that is, alternative weapons designs. If the requirements-
validation process has been carried out properly, a solid
basis for competition should have been developed. In Figure
5.6 the concept-definition process is shown to involve a comparative evaluation of detailed proposals (submitted in response to a request for proposals), including documented cost
and risk analysis. It also involves reevaluation of the effectiveness of the proposed systems against projected threats
or in terms of mission goals, and assessment of the validity of
cost and risk analyses and of management factors such as the
past experience of the contractors. In the case of acquisition
strategies involving subsystem as well as system-level proposals, the system-integration aspects must also be considered.

The end products of this phase are the selection of one
or more proposed options for demonstration, and documentation of a plan for the validation and demonstration phase in a
decision coordination paper (DCP).

It is clear from the foregoing that the management
strategy of the concept-formulation phase must be tailored to
the specific nature of the program. The degree of technical
risk of projected concepts, the impact of the operational environment on performance, the level of system complexity,
and integration requirements differ widely among development
programs. These factors, along with the maturity of the applicable technology base, and whether the mission need may
be met by evolutionary changes in existing systems, determine the optimum contracting strategy to be pursued and the
appropriate roles of defense R&D centers in support of the
program.

In the formal process of concept definition, the mission-
oriented centers generally serve as technical support to the
program manager in the formulation of the request for proposal, in operational and technical evaluation of contractor
proposals, and preparation for DSARC I. In the case of in-
house centers, government employees can also serve as members of the program management organization and participate
in the actual contractor-selection process.

FEEDBACK FROM DEVELOPMENT, PRODUCTION, AND OPERATION

The program phases which follow concept formulation, beginning with the demonstration and validation phase (also referred to as advanced development), consume far more effort
and cost than the conceptual phases, and involve difficult
problems and program decisions. (See Figure 5.3.) The
course of these latter phases depends critically on the thor-
oughness of the analyses and quality of the earlier decisions
made in verifying the mission element need, defining a valid
operational requirement, and selecting one or more practical
system concepts capable of meeting the requirement. It is
likely that the largest single source of delays and cost overruns encountered in advanced and full-scale system development are changes late in the development cycle necessitated
by improper, inadequate, or unrealistic definition of operational requirements and insufficiently critical evaluation of
candidate system concepts. The impact of unanticipated
changes from this source is often even greater than that
resulting from changes necessitated by new intelligence of
enemy capabilities during the course of the program development cycle.

Inasmuch as this paper is concerned with the formative
stages of system acquisition, the succeeding paragraphs consider these later phases only in terms of the information feedback from them to mission need and concept formulation for

modified or follow-on weapon systems (see Figure 5.4), a
process in which defense R&D centers play a particularly important role.

Demonstration and Validation Phase

The objective of the demonstration and validation phase of the
system-acquisition cycle is to develop the system concepts
selected in the concept-formulation phase to the point where a
decision may be made with confidence to proceed to full-scale
engineering development. Surprises are to be expected in
the new technology areas, but they are also often encountered in what were believed to be straightforward applications
of established techniques. Furthermore, if the conceptual
phases have not been done properly, the demonstration phase
will uncover deficiencies in requirements or technical approaches which will necessitate substantial changes in design
and consequent delays in the program. Indeed, the express
purpose of the demonstration and validation phase is to uncover such deficiencies at a relatively early stage, where
appropriate changes in requirements and approaches may be
introduced with minimal disruption of the program schedule or
increase in overall costs. An important collateral result is
the increase in understanding by the service sponsor and the
system developer of the relation of what may be desirable to
what is practically achievable, a process which constitutes a
valuable feedback for the concept and definition of follow-on
systems. The institutional memory inherent in defense R&D
centers is an important factor for making this feedback
effective.

Full-Scale Development

When a major program reaches the stage of full-scale engineering development, system design must be effectively frozen
and strict change and interface control imposed. However, in
any new complex system requiring many years to develop,
such events as unexpected increases in the threat, changes
in military plans, advent of new materials and devices, and
unanticipated difficulties in the transition to a producible
design, all introduce problems requiring quick resolution
before severe schedule and cost slippages occur. The main
burden for solving these problems falls on the contractor's
engineering organization. In addition, in order to review and
approve any specification, schedule, or cost changes as may
be required, the program management organization must also
be expert and well staffed, either organically or by relying
on an R&D center to provide general-systems-engineering and

integration-support functions. The technical breadth and
understanding of user needs possessed by the defense R&D
centers is especially valuable in anticipating and resolving
conflicts between performance requirements and system reliability, cost, or schedule.

Operation

During the operational phase, industry participation is generally limited to service support in the field, when called upon.
In-service engineering support for many major programs is
provided by in-house R&D centers or engineering support
centers. This function, which may extend throughout the
lifetime of the system, involves the solution of problems encountered because of unforeseen effects of the operational
environment on system performance and reliability. It also
may involve support and analysis of operational exercises
conducted under simulated combat conditions. Both provide
knowledge valuable in the formulation of follow-on systems.

Feedback to Mission Needs and System Concepts

In the formulation of mission needs and system concepts to
meet such needs, it is essential that their foundation be firm-
ly based on experience with the hard, practical realities of
technical limitations as well as possibilities, requirements of
reliability and cost as well as performance, and the complex-
ities of the operational environment in which military systems
must perform - including the service personnel who must
operate them. This experience can only come from direct
participation in the development, production, and operational
phases of weapons systems. In the case of evolutionary systems, continuity and feedback of experience is often provided
by the principal industrial contractors. In many areas the
cradle-to-grave involvement of R&D centers with major military systems provides an experience base and institutional
memory unavailable elsewhere. In these instances, the process of formulating new mission-element needs and system
concepts should be so structured that the relevant experience
base which has been built up by R&D centers and industry is
fully utilized.

SUMMARY

A major weapons or communication system for the U.S. military services will take five to ten years for full development,

will be in production for perhaps a decade, will have a useful
life of two to three decades, and may cost $30 billion to de-
velop and produce, and require a comparable expenditure for
its lifetime operation and maintenance. Clearly it becomes of
the utmost importance to choose well and design carefully.
Perhaps the most important stages in the entire acquisition
process for these systems are the initial ones, the establishment of a need for a new system and the consequent development of an appropriate conceptual response to the need.
The starting point is the operational requirements of the military services. One must examine these in the light of current mission responses, possible system improvements, and
the potential of new and more effective responses using new
technology.

The nonprofit defense R&D centers are uniquely qualified
to play a key role in these initial stages of system development. They serve to bring together information on requirements and on current system effectiveness. Working interactively with the military, the industrial production units,
and the originators of new technologies, they can help develop alternative solutions to the operational needs, study
these from the standpoint of cost effectiveness, and make
recommendations on preferred solutions. Their nonprofit
status encourages the objectivity which is essential for their
"bridging" role.

Recent OMB and DOD regulations and directives have
formalized the decision processes for the formulation of mission needs and conceptual responses as well as for the later
stages in system acquisition. These directives lead to a desirable sense of order and explicitness in the decision
making. However, there is frequently a large cost from red
tape, indecision, and delay. It is extremely desirable for the
federal government to find procedures which will result in the
desired responsibility and care in decision making, and yet
give the program manager sufficient flexibility to tailor acquisition strategy to his specific needs and the potential for
innovation, to ensure that the new systems are both responsive to mission needs and are obtained in timely fashion.

NOTES

(1) See Kenneth A. Boyd, "A Discussion of the Responsi-
     bilities and Functions of the Navy Research Development
     Centers," Naval Engineers Journal, December 1978, pp.
     63-66.
(2) Norman Waks, "The Honest Broker," The MITRE Cor-
     poration, Bedford, Massachusetts, 1978, pp. 1-6.

(3)   The Report to the President on Government   Contracting
      for Research and Development   (Washington   D.C.:   U.S.
      Government   Printing   Office),   April   30,   1962   by   the
      Presidential Committee headed by David E. Bell, Director
      of the Budget, was one of the first major studies of
      government   R&D   operations.   The Report of the Task
      Group on Defense In-house Laboratories,   July   1,   1971
      for the Deputy Secretary of Defense and the Director of
      Defense Research and Engineering, was one of the more
      substantive of the many studies of DOD in-house labo-
      ratories and their functions.

IV
The R & D Process

6 American Styles of Military R & D*

Robert Perry

"R&D style" is the accepted designation for the policies, procedures, and preferences that characterize research and development programs. There is, in concept, an American style and a Soviet style. American military R&D is often alleged to be wasteful, ill managed, and marred by cost overruns, performance shortfalls, and schedule slippages. Depending on the preconceptions of the viewers, Soviet military R&D may be characterized as sound and productive, hidebound and lackluster, or imaginative and fruitful. Most observers agree that it is well funded and abundantly staffed, but that its quality is less certain.

Such images largely derive from American perceptions of the post-Sputnik Soviet-American R&D competition, although some observations stem from still more ancient criticisms of American military R&D.(1)

_____

*I am indebted to Giles Smith, Michael Rich, Mark Lorell, and Alvin Harman of Rand for suggestions that influenced this paper. I may also have made off with some of their words, having annexed their research. But the views expressed here are ultimately my own. In an abbreviated version, this chapter was prepared for and orally presented at a March 1979 conference on military R&D sponsored by Cornell University and the Rockefeller Foundation, as part of a comparison of Soviet and U.S. R&D styles. As noted elsewhere, David Holloway prepared a companion piece on the Soviet Union. The research summarized here was supported by the Rand Corporation, in the public interest, and draws on findings earlier reported to various clients. None of those institutions necessarily subscribe to my conclusions or observations.

The image and the reality have little in common. In both countries civil R&D differs from military R&D in so many respects that to each must be attributed its own special features. Within the American defense establishment, the Army, Navy, and Air force favor different methods of conducting and managing R&D.(2) The Soviet Air Force, Navy, armored forces, strategic missile forces, and military space programs display a somewhat narrower but still diverse set of style preferences. Within the U.S. Air Force, aircraft, spacecraft, and large electronic systems are developed in ways that differ substantially, as do the several institutions directly responsible for them. At what many consider the level of the least common denominator - the industrial firms that contract for military R&D - differences may be less obvious but no less pronounced: the fashion in which the Lockheed California Company's advanced development organization conducts military R&D projects is as distinctive as the name it carries - "the skunk works" - and as formidable of reputation. But the skunk works style is readily distinguishable from that of the Lockheed Sunnyvale organization (which develops military spacecraft), and neither resembles that of the Northrop fighter aircraft design group in Hawthorne, California, some 20 miles south, or the nearby McDonnell-Douglas group that is responsible for civil transport programs.

Perhaps most important, R&D styles change with time, and not always for the worse.

Here, then, are themes to be developed and questions to be explored. Is there, or has there historically been, a typical American style of R&D? If so, is it changing, and how? Is there a typical Soviet style of R&D to which it can be compared? What are the differences, and how or why are they important? And, at the end, does one or the other have an advantage?

What has been said earlier supports the premise that if there is a distinctive American style of military R&D, it lacks definition and varies from place to place as well as from time to time. Conceivably, the "style" of a group immediately charged with responsibility for an R&D program could influence R&D outcomes more than the formal usages of the sponsoring service or department; thus any generalization about U.S. military R&D should take account of the extreme diversity of R&D approaches encompassed in the many sets and subsets of American R&D programs and projects. Style characterizations are therefore likely to apply only to small lots of similar programs.

Traditionally, many of the "successful" and "unsuccessful" outcomes of various R&D undertakings are attributed to differences of R&D style. Indeed, having attempted to evaluate the influences of many other variables on R&D program outcomes, expounders on the theory and practice of R&D are frequently driven to accept "style" as a best explanation of success or failure.(3)   Nothing else seems to serve as well.

The principal style elements of successful military R&D, whenever conducted and by whomever, probably can be epitomized in three broad propositions. First and most important, the management of an R&D enterprise must be responsive to the contemporary state and nature of whatever technology is being manipulated. One discriminator is whether "large" advances in system performance can be extracted from a particular R&D program. Will the state of the technology being exploited support an attempt to leap grandly ahead, or should ambition be limited to smaller and presumably more realistic advances?(4)   In the end, it would seem that successful new weapons more often derive from proven technology than from efforts to shape, push, or contrive immature technology – however well intentioned, well funded, or well managed those efforts may be. History says that technology shapes requirements far more often than requirements effectively pull technology. It follows, then, that the rate at which a given technology is advancing may determine the outcome of an R&D enterprise – but that rate of change is little affected by such factors as pulsations in budget levels or program priorities, the skill and dedication of program managers, or the forceful intercessions of a service secretary.

Second, the fundamental goal of R&D is to reduce uncertainty, but uncertainty cannot always be diminished fast enough to ensure program "success." Therefore cancellation must be viewed as one acceptable outcome of <u>any</u> R&D project, sometimes vastly preferable to a calculated continuing effort to achieve the unachievable. In some instances remarkable technical accomplishments result from determined assaults on uncertainty, but (as in the recent cases of the Anglo-French and Russian supersonic transports) there may be some lingering doubt that the game was worth the candle.

Third, an unqualified commitment to some monolithic concept, approach, or means of performing some desired function can inculcate a costly failure or a yet more costly "success"; for example, the late delivery of expensive military equipment which proves to be of little or no military worth. The several German "V-weapons" of 1944-1945 are striking examples, although some more recent cases can be found.

Some of the perceived differences between Soviet and U.S. R&D approaches derive from culture, tradition, and dogma. For example, it is a Soviet credo that weaponry (which is to say, technology) cannot drive military strategy, but rather that doctrine determines requirements which in turn dictate technology choices. It is somewhat surprising that recent discussions of Soviet R&D style(5) which include that aspect do not remark that one who is required to honor the dogma that doctrine drive technology, but observes that it does not, will ordinarily prefer conservative technology in responding to requirements. Even the most doctrinaire Russian R&D specialists must have noticed that demanding some technical achievement does not have the desired effect unless the requisit technology is ready to hand. Clever reintegration of proven technology, frequent small advances, and demonstration of system capability before commitment to operational service characterized Soviet aircraft and tracked-vehicle development from the 1930s at least into the 1960s. Recent Russian departures from those patterns have had unhappy consequences. The exceptionally long delay in availability of the Soviet Il.86 wide-body civil transport and the complete failure of the Tu.144 supersonic transport program are cases in point.(6)   Because all Russian aerospace programs can be treated as extensions of military R&D enterprise, it is likely that similar failures have occurred in similar military programs. Soviet military security would have prevented their coming to public notice.

For at least the past decade, the Soviets have been credited with having extensively exploited the traditional advantages of incremental development. A leading spokesman for that view has been Arthur Alexander, who has pointed out the benefits of incrementalism, cost consciousness, and design conservatism - which the United States often forgoes in enthusiasm for new technology.(7)   Alexander Flax has argued that such generalizations oversimplify several important issues. He takes the position that Soviet R&D authorities have been as technologically ambitious as their American counterparts and that Americans consistently and effectively exploit incrementalism.(8)   David Holloway has observed that Soviet designers and R&D managers, even at the highest military and political levels, apparently prefer to invest in design improvement and incrementalism if that is possible; but in instances when doctrinal goals cannot be so satisfied, "Manhattan Project" enterprise styles may be adopted.(9)   In such instances, Soviet technology has been hard pressed to maintain the pace required of it.

This would be heady stuff for graduate school seminars if it were not so vital a determinant of the comparative military readiness of the two countries. Is Soviet style no more than incrementalism leavened by random breakthrough efforts? Is it the other face of the American coin? Does it matter?

One approach to such questions is to begin with the assumption that there is a nationally preferred Soviet R&D style, although (as with Soviet military doctrine) expediency, pragmatism, and "special circumstances" may condition Soviet responses to particular challenges. Further, it seems obvious that in a great many ways the customary Soviet R&D approach in, for instance, tank development is different from the way the Soviets developed their earliest ballistic missiles. But it is also conceivable that the present Soviet preference for product improvement in ballistic missiles may be no more than a new expression of the Soviet tradition of incremental development.

Institutional inertia makes it unlikely that one approach can quickly be substituted for another in Soviet military R&D; thus, a rapid shift from incrementalism to concurrency would be difficult. The conventional, safest, most acceptable, most familiar, and therefore the institutionally preferred Soviet approach is incrementalism.(10)   But on occasion, circumstances compel the Soviets to attempt to ingest large quantities of risky technology to match or offset new systems and concepts introduced by the Americans (sub-launched ICBMs, MIRVs, and precision-guidance cruise missiles are examples). Dedicated and expensive efforts to advance technology on a schedule endorsed by the Kremlin have been unsuccessful in various respects (consider the SS-10 missile and the high-bypass turbofan engine, for example), partly because technology is no more respectful of commands sternly voiced in Russian than in English, but mostly because Soviet dogma, bureaucracy, and institutional and cultural rigidities impede Soviet efforts to perform the rapid programatic and funding starts, stops, and changes of direction that characterize - and are essential to the success of - the high-risk, high-technology aspects of U.S. military R&D.(11)

The best of American military R&D is characterized by pragmatism, adaptiveness, flexibility of approach, and a decent respect for the occasional intractability of technology. The striking advances often made by relatively small groups led by skillful, imaginative American innovators attract much attention.   But it is also true that much vital American military R&D depends on recurrent increments of performance improvement that are increasingly difficult to achieve. Who is to say that two decades of continuing small advances in the technology of the Sidewinder missile are of less military value than the spectacularly rapid creation of the F-16?

It seems safe to assume a present American advantage in some potentially critical areas of R&D enterprise, but an advantage that arises more in process and practice than in some broader mastery of the philosophy of R&D. Whether such an advantage can be extended or preserved remains uncertain. Russians have become keen students of the U.S. R&D management techniques to which the American advantage is often attributed.   But in their mix of R&D approaches, the Soviets still seem to be consistently less successful than the Americans. If Russian systems are cheaper, they also tend to be less advanced,(12) or at least, advanced in ways that the United States does not value as highly.   And the Soviets characteristically are slower to respond to newly perceived technical needs.

In some respects the persistence of an American R&D
advantage seems surprising; U.S. military R&D has malfunc-
tioned in many ways for many years. Although American R&D
managers typically respond to the identification of system-
specific problems by generating uniquely appropriate solutions, they also generalize from those solutions and apply
them indiscriminately to other systems with unrelated problems, thus creating new system-specific problems which then
require new unique solutions, and so on.

Rather than attempt to enumerate the problems, it seems
sufficient to list some of the solutions (Fig. 6.1) that have
been developed and applied, successfully or unsuccessfully,
by some sector of the American military in the past 15 or 20
years.

INSTITUTIONAL

Management Techniques

"Blue Line" (F-15)
Milestone Reviews
Reorganizations
Decisions at Ever Higher Levels:
    Secretary of Defense
    Congress
    The Presidency

Development Strategies

Concurrency (ICBM)
Multi-Service Weapons (F-111)
Fly-Before-Buy (A-10, UTTAS)
Prototyping (F-16/F-17)
Design-to-Cost

Test and Validation Variants

OSD Director for Test and
    Evaluation
Service Test Centers

PROCEDURAL

Planning

"Independent" Cost
    Estimates
Life Cycle Costing
Technical Risk
    Assessment
Cost Performance
    Tradeoff Models
Mission Element Need
    Statements

Contractual

Incentives
Cost Plus Fee
Fixed Price
Total Package
Warranties

Procurement

Profit Controls
Rewritten Procure-
    ment Regulations
"Set Asides"

Fig. 6.1 Solutions Attempted.

We already know that the routine application of "proven"
solutions to newly perceived problems more often complicates

than resolves them.   For example, the perception that con-
current development and production were advisable in the
terminal stages of ICBM programs of the late 1950s prompted
the view that routine compression and overlap of the sequential phases of all major acquisition programs could save time
and money.(13)   Translated into policy directives, that assumption eventually led to "total package procurement,"
which in application had mixed outcomes; to several tightly
compacted system-development programs with marginally useful
products; and to the near abandonment of such frequently
beneficial approaches as prototyping, extended testing, product improvement, and low-initial-rate production.   That the
inventiveness and energy of solution contrivers may be
flagging is implied by the recent revival of interest in concurrency, and by renewed arguments that prototyping and
proof testing are "too slow," "unnecessary," and "too costly."

Moving past the rubrics, the easy solutions, and the
panaceas brings one to a fundamental question: of what is
the R&D and acquisition process composed, and how is it
ordered?   The charts in Figures 6.2-6.4 depict its principal
elements as viewed from three different perspectives.   Figure
6.2, showing the conventional relationships among the various
phases,(14) reflects the assumption that each phase of acquisition is undertaken in sequence and is satisfactorily completed before another begins.

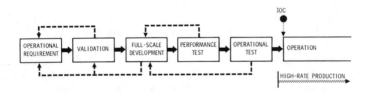

Fig. 6.2 Acquisition: the idealized conception.

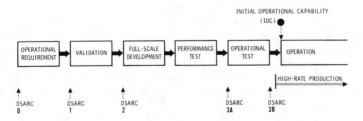

Fig. 6.3 Acquisition: the reality.

Figure 6.3 shows how development, test, validation, and production inevitably overlap and interact when program managers realistically address the main task of R&D: uncertainty reduction. Unless there is some compelling justification for risking cost overruns, schedule slippages, and system performance shortfalls, active feedback loops must interconnect the various activities. Realistic programs feature recurrent iteration because the reduction of risk and the accumulation of relevant new knowledge compel frequent reassessments of the relationships between requirements and technology, between design and test, and between operational validation and redesign. Industries dependent on technological advance routinely operate in accordance with such principles. No acquisition program that includes research and development can proceed successfully by way of a simple sequential process. One particularly important relationship is that operational tests should be satisfactorily completed before a commitment to high-rate production is made. There is, in the event, no other way of ensuring that standard production systems will perform as they are required to do after delivery to users.

The key to successful exploitation of the "realistic" mode of acquisition is the acknowledgement that any R&D progarm contains critical elements of risk and uncertainty. The insistence of program advocates that risk is minimal, or that all potential uncertainties have been anticipated and offset by procedural safeguards, is a routine predecessor of R&D difficulties.

Figure 6.4 represents the staging of acquisition functions in a fashion typical of American military R&D of the 1950s and 1960s. In many important programs, the interaction between operational requirements and technical validation was inadequate, encouraging a commitment to technically unrealistic goals. In the late phases of a program, an overlap of performance testing, operational testing, initial high-rate production, and actual service operations has been a classic response to schedule slippages that frequently originated in earlier technical difficulties. If test and production phases overlap to the extent that test findings cannot be applied to production articles, then costly factory, field, or depot modification programs may become the only feasible means of correcting latent flaws in the delivered item. Such an approach often means that early production systems will not satisfy either the original expectations or the current needs of the users. The interval between the official initial operational capability (IOC) date and the date of an effective operational capability may then be as much as two or three years. During that interval, systems may be hobbled by constraints on performance, or sidelined to await modification. If the cost of advisable modifications exceeds the resources

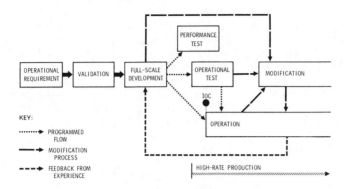

Fig. 6.4.   Acquisition: the concurrency approach.

available, the expected operational capability may never by fully achieved. One classic example is the A-7D aircraft, planned for a sortie rate in excess of three per day, but which when delivered proved capable of only one sortie per day. In effect, the Air Force either paid three times as much as it expected to pay for the A-7D's sortie capability or received only one-third of the capability it paid for.

Although program cancellation is - conceptually at least - an alternative to the production of a flawed system, political, technical, or military considerations may make it infeasible. In such cases, some compromise of performance becomes the only real option.

One classic means of reconciling inadequate technological capabilities with excessively ambitious requirements statements was illustrated by the F-111 (TFX) program. Only if highly optimistic expectations of technical progress had been realized could the 69,000-pound F-111 (designed in 1962) have provided the combination of supersonic dash and extended mission radius that its designers - and purchasers - expected. Mostly because of weight increases (to 82,000 pounds) during development, the aircraft that was finally produced lacked that capacity. But without those weight compromises, the F-111 would have had no useful operational capability. An F-111 of 69,000 pounds could be flown only about 100 miles at Mach 1.2 - and at that point its fuel would have been exhausted.

The C-5A experience provides an example of the consequences of not making reasonable compromises during development. Although the aircraft was to be a very modest advance in the state of the art, the C-5A program was eventually acknowledged to be a highly ambitious technological enterprise. A major goal of the original program was to deliver two main battle tanks to NATO on an unrefueled mission over 2,800 nautical miles. The C-5A as delivered could perform that task. But the C-5A was tightly constrained by design speci- fications embedded in the contract, precluding most trade- offs:(15) About 14,000 pounds of airframe structure had to be removed to reconcile takeoff distance, gross weight, and fixed empty-weight requirements. Most came from the wing. Sub- sequently the Air Force concluded that the main structure had been so greatly weakened in the process that service life expectancy had been unacceptably reduced. If present plans (1979) are carried out and a "new" wing is retrofitted to all C-5A aircraft, the deleted 14,000 pounds will be restored. The cost is likely to exceed $1.3 billion (1977 dollars), and unless performance compensations can somehow be provided, the modified aircraft will be unable to perform the mission for which it was designed.(16) The product of a determined ef- fort to satisfy unachievable technical goals on an accelerated schedule was the delivery of a gravely flawed system at a cost greatly in excess of estimates for what was once alleged to be an "off-the-shelf" design.

One contributor to the outcomes of such programs as the F-111 and C-5A appears to have been premature commitment to high-rate production. Typically, in the 1960s, both the decision to begin high-rate production and the actual start of production preceded the completion of either development or operational testing (performance validation), and frequently preceded the start of operational tests.(17) Such early com- mitment to high-rate production interferes with or even pre- cludes the effective feedback of test findings into the design (and redesign) of the production article. In such instances, the performance of the delivered article may be appreciably inferior to that sought when the program was approved. A common consequence is the costly and extensive modification of the delivered system, or the delivery of an incapable or marginally capable system, or both.

Although schedule compression and some degree of con- currency typified many DOD acquisition programs of the 1960s, that was not always the case. Perhaps the most ob- vious example of a shift from traditional incremental-develop- ment and product-improvement strategies to a "more modern" concept has been in the acquisition of tanks for the U.S. Army.

Since its beginnings in the 1920s, Soviet tank develop- ment has relied on the continual improvement of some exist- ing, well-tested armored vehicle. Until the early 1960s, U.S. tank development was also conventionally reliant on a product- improvement strategy. Then, in a belated conversion to the "total system" concept originated by the Air Force, Army R&D philosophy changed (see Fig. 6.5). Thereafter, the goal of Army R&D was to design mostly new tanks from the ground up.(18)   Perhaps it is fortunate that traditions of product improvement could not be instantaneously dispensed with, because in more than ten years of trying, the "total system" concept did not bring on an "all new" production tank. Indeed – and in the event; fortunately – a further improved version of the M-60 (of 1959 vintage) was entered into production after the "new" tank concept was adopted.

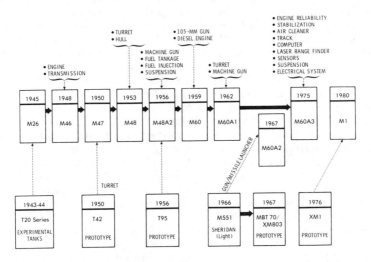

Fig. 6.5.   How U.S. heavy tanks were developed.

One potential explanation for the difficulty of developing a "total system" tank may be that breakthrough technology is not an applicable option in tank development.   Improvements come so slowly there, and radical advances so infrequently, that only derivative designs are compatible with cost-effective progress.(19)   Another difficulty is that institutions accustomed to incrementalism cannot quickly accommodate to new ways of doing things – a constraint that applies to 50-year-old Soviet tank-design institutions as much as to their American equivalents.

Major institutional pressures on the U.S. military R&D process have been generated by assumptions about what endangers an approved program.   A common argument against incrementalism as an R&D strategy is that it delays production approval.   It is widely believed in the military that new equipment designs constitute a more effective hedge against an uncertain technological future than "improved" versions of older systems or subsystems.   And tests often are directed at establishing <u>how</u> components will perform rather than <u>how</u>

well, or how long, or whether an integration of newly developed components will function effectively at all. Proponents of breakthrough-style R&D maintain that it is not necessary to address such questions before production approvals have been granted, and that attempting to answer them all before scheduling a production start can delay or even prevent progress toward operational availability.

For what then seemed to be good reasons, an R&D strategy featuring compressed schedules, overlapping phases, and "total system" concepts was generally adopted by the Air Force in the 1950s and was either adopted by or imposed on the other services in the 1960s. The usual program outcomes included cost growth, schedule slips, and performance shortfalls. Some of the remedies - the "solutions" alluded to earlier - were contrived to mitigate the consequences of performance and schedule shortcomings. Frequently, they worsened the situation. Very real concern about the state of defense R&D was voiced by the late 1960s. In itself, that was nothing new or unusual, but a greater pragmatism became apparent in changes that were proposed thereafter. Whatever their inspiration may have been, R&D policy changes adopted in the early 1970s came to be known as the Packard initiatives, after Deputy Secretary of Defense David Packard, one of the more outspoken advocates of fundamental reform in the defense acquisition process.

What were these changes, and what was their effect? for answers we can turn to a recent examination of 32 major systems(20) that entered full-scale development during the 1970s. Together, the systems in the sample accounted for more than $100 billion of DOD investment in research, development, production, and initial support.

A major policy initiative to emerge from experience of the 1960s was emphasis on tests of actual hardware in lieu of theoretical analyses and "paper studies"; hardware demonstrations became increasingly prevalent after 1969. Indeed, 80 percent of the programs in the sample and all major programs that started after 1973 included some hardware testing before the start of full-scale development. To the extent that the data can be assessed, the availability of hardware test results seems to have been a considerable factor in approving or disapproving the start of full-scale development. Figure 6.6 shows a pronounced trend toward the increased generation of test data as the decade wore on.(21)

Greater reliance on hardware competition in selecting systems for full-scale development and in deciding when they were ready for production was another major initiative of the early 1970s. Although virtually unknown during the 1960s and only gradually effective in the early 1970s, hardware competition occurred in the predevelopment phases of two-thirds of the major systems that entered acquisition after

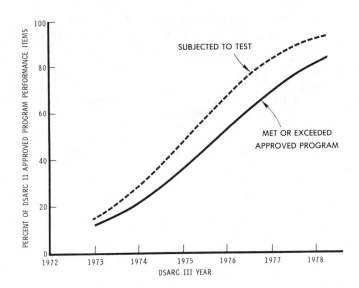

Fig. 6.6.   Trends in performance testing.

1973. Between 1969 and 1974, only 30 percent of the new acquisition programs included hardware competition during the years before full-scale development began.

In three important categories, then, the process changes introduced by David Packard actually took effect. Hardware demonstration became a regular feature of system development of the 1970s, performance testing showed a pronounced increase, and hardware competition became much more prevalent after 1973. Although the sample is small and the data are not extensive, the trends seem clear enough.

Were the effects of such changes beneficial, and if so, in what respects? Did they impose important new costs on the acquisition process? Did they lower performance standards, delay completion of programs, or make products less cost effective?

To determine the consequences of conducting acquisitions under the terms of the new practices requires examining the extent to which program cost, schedule, and system performance outcomes departed from the goals and objectives ("predicted program outcomes") accepted by the sponsoring service and the developer at the time full-scale development began.(22)

Consider hardware competition. Where it occurred, what was its value? One way of evaluating effects is to compare

actual with projected goals for programs that involved significant hardware competition during development and for programs that did not. The comparison must extend to total
acquisition cost, development schedules, and system performance.

The results? The four programs in the sample that included hardware competition (AWACS, A-10, F-16, and UH-60)
incurred substantially less cost growth and significantly fewer
schedule slips than programs that did not involve substantial
hardware competition (F-15, Aegis, Harpoon, AIM-9L, Captor,
and M-198). (See Table 6.1.) System performance differences were not significant. Such indicators should be treated
cautiously because of the small size of the sample, but the
implications are provocative: where hardware competition occurred, it seemed to pay dividends.

Table 6.1:   Some Effects of Hardware Competition

	With Competitive Hardware	Without Competitive Hardware
Actual Outcome/Approved Program		
Total Acquisition Cost	1.16	1.53
Development Schedule . . . . (Months from DSARC II to Milestone)	1.08	1.22
Approved Program/Actual Outcome		
System Performance	.98	1.07

A different but equally encouraging effect of hardware
competition was observed in several programs in which full-
scale system prototypes were built and tested before or
during full-scale development. In three instances (A-X, the
Lightweight Fighter, and the Advanced Attack Helicopter),
test program participants were convinced that the design that
won the prototype hardware flyoff competitions would not
have been selected had only paper designs been evaluated.
Although not quantifiable, the effect of building competing
prototype systems before full-scale development was to select
a "better" system. In any case, hardware testing - prototyping - seems to be beneficial.

Without considering (for the moment) what the causes or
trends may be in the 32 programs here sampled, cost growth

(the excess of incurred costs over planned costs, in constant dollars) averaged 20 percent, exceeded 100 percent in one instance, and was negative in three instances. Over the first eight years after the start of full-scale development, cost growth averaged 5.6 percent per year. Larger - more expensive - programs incurred proportionately less cost growth than small programs. One obvious explanation for the continuing cost growth trend lies in the unpredictability of R&D: older programs incur more cost growth than newer ones because they are exposed to larger numbers of unpredicted events over time.

This prompts the question of whether cost growth is more pronounced during development or during production. Conventional wisdom holds the former to be more common, but most of the seven production programs in the sample exhibited growth during both phases (see Fig. 6.7.) The most obvious exception, the UH-60 helicopter, was also the only program in the entire sample in which direct competition between two contractors was maintained throughout full-scale development. That is particularly interesting, given the earlier indications of the benefits of competition, but not too much should be made of a sample of one.

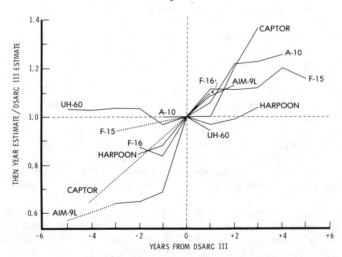

Fig. 6.7. Program cost trends in
development and production.

Since 1969, program schedules have been about 13 percent longer than anticipated, although in a few instances program milestone achievements took twice as long as had been planned. System performance departures from initial plan were few: the average system in the 32 programs in the

sample achieved its performance goals, but individual vari-
ances ranged from half as "good" to twice as "good" as expected.(23)

As compared to some recent civil projects (like the Alas-
kan pipeline, which cost about five times as much and took
twice as long as promised), the defense programs in the sample appear to have done rather well. Further, all of the comparisons made thus far suggest that the policy changes insti-
tuted in the early 1970s, prompted by several studies of
flawed policies of the 1960s, had beneficial effects in particular areas.

But were overall program outcomes of the 1970s "better"
than those of the 1960s? Can one say with confidence that
prototyping, increased testing, more careful program review,
and greater program competition paid off in terms in schedule, cost, and system performance?

A baseline for such comparisons exists. In 1969, a Rand
study team compared the actual to the predicted outcomes of
24 DOD acquisition programs of the 1960s. Although smaller
than the more recent sample and containing a different mix of
systems, it is nonetheless comparable. Techniques that permit researchers to correct for differences in the technical difficulty of programs in the two decades do not exist, so inter-
decade comparisons of schedule and cost growth trends may
be mildly suspect. Moreover, changes in ratios of actual to
predicted outcomes may derive from shifts in the value of the
numerator or the denominator, or both. That is, a perceived
reduction in typical cost growth could be the product of
better cost control, or of better estimating, or of some combination of the two. Small differences could signify little.

But average cost growth in programs of the 1970s has
been only half of that experienced by systems of the 1960s
(20 percent rather than 40 percent).(24) Relatively smaller
differences existed in scope of schedule slip and system performance.(25) All differences between the 1960s and the
1970s show the later decade to have been "better" (see Table
6.2).

Because the sample from the 1960s contained no development programs less than three years old, similar "young" programs were deleted from the 1970s sample. That adjustment
raised the average cost growth increase for the 1970s to a
factor of 1.34, not much better than the 1.40 of the 1960s.
But when the ratio of actual to anticipated values is recalcu-
lated in terms of the total costs for all programs in the sample (thus weighting for program size), the "mature" 1970s
programs sample shows a growth ratio of 1.20, less than half
that of the 1960s (1.47). That difference is impressive.
Finally, when the two samples are adjusted to equalize program age, the 1970s programs show real annual cost growth
rate 25-percent lower than the 1960s. (That is, 5.6 percent

Table 6.2. Inter-decade Comparisons

	Actual Outcome/Approved Program (Average of Complete Samples)	
	1960s	1970s
Total Acquisition Cost	1.40	1.20
With "Young" Programs Deleted	1.40	1.34
Weighted for Program Size	1.47	1.20
Development Schedule	1.15	1.13
(Months from DSARC II to Milestone)		
System Performance	1.05	1.00
Annual Cost Growth Rate (above inflation)	7.4%	5.6%

in the 1970s against 7.4 percent in the 1960s.) Thus there can be no doubt that, since 1970, significant improvements have occurred in the predictability or the control of program costs, or both. Owing to peculiarities in the data, it is not possible to demonstrate that the improvement is more nearly 60 percent (the apparent upper bound) than 30 percent. But at the least, the net constant-dollar value of the improvement is more than $10 billion for the 32 systems in the sample. However that may be accounted or apportioned, it is no insignificant sum.

Has that achievement cost something not captured in the calculation? One issue prominent in discussions of acquisition policy in 1979 is the length of time today needed to complete a program. The difficulty of doing much with the question arises in defining, and then determining for each of many systems of recent decades, when development began and when it ended. The excursion attempted here considers aircraft programs of the past 30 years.

Two caveats: First, the sample contains only aircraft systems. A comparably adequate set of data covering missiles or armored vehicles or other significant pieces of military hardware apparently does not exist.(26) Second, the survey concerns only that portion of the acquisition cycle that occurred after the beginning of full-scale development (as currently defined).(27) Although some other studies have concluded that acquisition programs lengthened in the 1970s because of delays in decisions during planning and concept formulation phases, the data available for this comparison would not support findings on that score.

For the evaluation, the acquisition time histories of 37 aircraft were measured from the start of full-scale development, to first flight of the first airplane model produced under the development contract, and to delivery of the first operational item to an operational squadron.

Three recent prototype programs (A-10, F-16, F-18) complicate the assessment of program initiation. By one mode of measurement, the start of prototype development marks program start, although formal full-scale development did not actually start until DSARC Milestone II, which followed prototype demonstration and final source selection.(28)

Using the early start dates for the three prototype programs produces results which show that both time to first flight and total development time (reflected in time to first delivery of an operational aircraft) increased slightly over the past 30 years. If DSARC II dates are taken to indicate program start points for the three recent prototype programs, the results suggest that average total development time decreased modestly during the three decades and that time to first flight remained constant.

Extending the time measurement to include delivery of the first 200 operational aircraft is also complicated by alternative interpretations of the start dates for the recent prototype aircraft programs. The pessimistic interpretation of the data shows that total acquisition times (including a substantial production phase) have increased by about 25 percent for aircraft systems in the past 35 years. But if DSARC II start dates are used for the two recent prototype programs,(29) a flat trend line results.

Some decrease in average production rates is also evident. That is not surprising, considering that current aircraft are as much as ten times more expensive (in terms of unit cost as a fraction of the total acquisition budget) and three to five times as heavy as comparable aircraft of the 1940s and early 1950s. In terms of constant dollars or pounds of aircraft per unit of time, however, production rates have not appreciably decreased during the past 30 years.

If, therefore, the total time needed to acquire new aircraft has been somewhat extended since the end of World War II, the change must be mostly credited to lower production rates. Other available data indicate that derivative aircraft take less time in development than entirely new designs, but that is not likely to surprise anyone. And, of course, the available data do not support any conclusions about trends in the time required to proceed from system concept (or some similar milestone) to approval for development. As yet, a data base and measurement methodology appropriate for such calculations are lacking.

OBSERVATIONS

If the American military R&D style is difficult to categorize or to define, it is at least possible to suggest that outcomes have improved in recent years, that the process works reasonably well, and that by all the standards we can apply, it is increasingly effective. It is changing, in considerable part, because the Department of Defense has largely abandoned efforts to order up technology without regard for costs. Caution and risk aversion seem to be more pronounced both in selecting new systems and in committing to production. Consider that for various reasons, mostly quite sound, the B-1 and the American SST were cancelled. Somewhere in Russia the people who ordered the Tu.144 into production may envy the disorderly, unruly R&D style that led to such abortive developments.

American military R&D style is characteristically inconsistent in many aspects. It includes both derivative designs and innovative ones. For both, practitioners have (recently, at least) become rather adept at selecting and exploiting advanced technology suited to the needs of the time. Few major U.S. military development programs of recent vintage have required great inventive leaps into the unknown for success; on the contrary, the Department of Defense has increasingly invested in early hardware testing, and all the evidence says the benefits have been substantial. If postponement or cancellation of prominent but disappointing U.S. programs occurs less often today, it may be that fewer inappropriate programs progress far enough into development to invoke such Draconian measures. American R&D managers appear to have become better judges of the likelihood that a given rate of technological progress can be maintained. And they have become more adept at creating and preserving desirable technological options. This is not to say that all is well in the halls of military technology, or that further improvement is not needed. But the sky is not falling.

Whether Soviet or American, R&D institutions as readily aspire to organizational immortality as do trade guilds or cavalry regiments; instinctively, they resist change. In general, the USSR prefers an R&D process that proceeds from the orderly improvement of previously developed systems, and for the last 35 years the United States has preferred starting systems from scratch and seeking bold technical advances. Of course there are exceptions to both generalizations, and in the American case, styles are changing. Several political and institutional factors inhibit the Soviet creation of new R&D or production organizations and encourage the continuance of established institutions that favor an R&D style based more on derivatives than new initiatives. A tightly integrated planning structure, centralized resource allocation, and unwillingness to countenance unemployment tend to inhibit quick changes of process, product, or approach in Soviet military R&D. If the need is sufficiently great, the Soviets (with undisguisable difficulty) establish new enterprises; when the benefits of incrementalism appreciably diminish, they reluctantly invest in wholly new designs. The United States innovates more skillfully, more routinely, and with less anguish. The Soviets appear to lack the doctrinal and procedural flexibility that is characteristic of American military R&D. With all its impediments, the American system is astonishingly resilient, able to survive rapid starts and stops and changes of direction, scope, or goal. It accommodates effectively to technical, financial, and procedural "instability" notwithstanding the noisy complaints of some who would prefer a less certain future and a more monolithic institution. Skillful managers are able to create new initiatives and to compose alternative goals, to reallocate resources, and to exploit unheralded technology. Such opportunities are not automatically provided by the more doctrinaire R&D institutions of the Soviet Union, even if those units are more generously funded and more heavily staffed. In areas where technology is changing rapidly, where new initiatives are frequent, where both payoff and risk are potentially large, the U.S. military R&D style, whatever its shortcomings, has a decided advantage over that of the Soviet Union. At the end, one is tempted to paraphrase a comment on democracy attributed to Churchill: Our's is the worst possible way of doing R&D - except for all the others.

NOTES

(1)   The literature on American and Russian R&D styles is abundant and of varied quality. A well-known study that epitomizes informed opinion of the late 1960s is Arthur J. Alexander, R&D in Soviet Aviation, R-589 (Santa Monica, Cal.: Rand Corporation, November 1970). The standard reference on American military R&D at mid-century is M. J. Peck and F. J. Scherer, The Weapons Acquisition Process: An Economic Analysis (Cambridge: Harvard University Press, 1962). One of the several attempts to examine the two institutions as they were in the late 1960s is Robery Perry, Comparisons of Soviet and U.S. Technology, R-827 (Santa Monica, Cal.: Rand Corporation, June 1973).

(2) The widely used and somewhat misleading generaliza-
     tions for the three service "styles" are (respectively),
     "arsenal," "bureau," and "contract" R&D.
(3) The Polaris ballistic missile and the Navaho cruise mis-
     sile programs of roughly the same era are useful exam-
     ples.
(4) For illustrative purposes: the development of the first
     supersonic bomber may represent a "large" advance; the
     development of a 10 percent "better" inertial-guidance
     system for a ballistic missile may represent a "small"
     advance. This is not to say that one will be intrinsic-
     ally more likely to succeed than the other. If the tech-
     nology essential to a supersonic bomber is at hand, the
     program has a large potential for success; if a 10 per-
     cent improvement in guidance accuracy requires a level
     of precision in gyroscope stability that cannot be
     achieved, that project may well fail.
(5) See, for instance, Col. R. G. Head, "Technology and
     the Military Balance," Foreign Affairs, April 1978; and
     Arthur J. Alexander, Decision-Making in Soviet Weapons
     Procurement, Adelphi Paper No. 147 (London: Interna-
     tional Institute for Strategic Studies, 1978).
(6) It is an interesting commentary on the quality of three
     different R&D styles that the United States abandoned
     its infant SST program as soon as a government subsidy
     of costly, high-risk technology was withdrawn; that
     Britain and France elected to proceed with economically
     calamitous compromises of technology in the prestigious
     but costly Concorde program; and that the Russians
     incurred economic and technological catastrophe as a
     consequence of ignoring both the American precept and
     the Russian tradition of technological conservatism.
(7) Alexander, Decision-Making in Soviet Weapons Procure-
     ment.
(8) Foreign Affairs, September 1978, pp. 207-211.
(9) "The Soviet Style of Military R&D," a paper prepared
     for the Cornell-Rockefeller Workshop, March 1979.
(10) Surprisingly, political scientists have not remarked on
     the chasm between Marxist R&D doctrine (innovative,
     unchained communist technology will overwhelm capital-
     ism) and recent Soviet R&D practice (conservative grad-
     ualism with an admixture of irrational adventurism).
(11) Robert Perry, "Verifying SALT in the 1980s," in C.
     Bertram, ed., The Future of Arms Control: Part 1, Be-
     yond SALT II, Adelphi Paper No. 141 (London: Interna-
     tional Institute for Strategic Studies, 1978), suggests
     that such institutional factors prevented the Soviets from
     successfully competing with the Americans in certain
     categories of strategic weapons development and that the
     Soviets would probably demand a cessation of American

R&D in some areas as a price for agreeing to reduction in strategic weapons inventories. Alternatively, the Soviets could extend and intensify their known efforts to adapt and exploit "American R&D management techniques" that would improve their ability to compete in areas of high-risk technology. Although the perplexing and self-contradictory nature of Soviet R&D has been the occasion for an enormous literature, a void remains; the policies, quality, and output of Soviet R&D deserve at least as much attention as has been devoted to the organization, infrastructure of, or resources consumed by, that institution.

(12) Notwithstanding disagreements about the comparative virtues of Russian and U.S. tanks, Foxbats and SR-71s, and U.S. and Russian jet engines, it appears to be generally acknowledged that U.S. systems both cost more and perform "better" - but differently.

(13) Compared to what? was treated as an unworthy question. When the assumption of cost savings proved unsupportable, the argument for concurrency became, "the time saving justifies the higher cost." In the event, analysis failed to provide much support for the assumption of schedule advantages. See B. H. Klein, T. K. Glennan, Jr., and G. H. Shubert, The Role of Prototypes in Development, RM-3467/1 (Santa Monica, Cal.: Rand Corporation, April 1971).

(14) For purposes of comparison, the five phases and subphases of the Defense System Acquisition Review Council (DSARC) approval process are shown. Phases 3A and 3B are, respectively, approvals for long lead time and high-rate production.

(15) Including costs. Each C-5A cost more than twice the original estimate, and in the end only half as many were built as the Air Force earlier said were needed.

(16) One obvious but expensive remedy would be to retrofit more powerful or more fuel-efficient engines, a measure Lockheed proposed before high-rate production began, but which was then turned down because it was inconsistent with the costs and operational schedules on which the "total package" contract was predicated. The most likely response would be to rely on aerial tankers for all full-load missions of more than about 2,200 nautical miles.

(17) The C-5A, F-111, A-10, and A-7D are examples.

(18) See Arthur J. Alexander, Armor Development in the Soviet Union and the United States, R-1860 (Santa Monica, Cal.: Rand Corporation, September 1976).

(19) Although technical obstacles have been common, the chief impediment to development of an "all new" tank has been its potential production cost.

(20)   The list includes:

Army		Navy		Air Force	
UH-60	HELLFIRE	AEGIS	LAMPS	F-15	ALCM/GLCM
M-198	AH-64	CAPTOR	SURTASS	B-1	
MICV/IFV	XM-1	AIM-7F	F-18	AWACS	
PATRIOT	DIVAD GUN	AIM-9L	TACTASS	A-10	
ROLAND		HARPOON	TOMAHAWK	F-16	
COPPERHEAD		CONDOR	5", 8" PROJECTILES	DSCS III	

Because this research was concerned with production systems, the many large ship-building programs of the Navy were deleted from the list.   Data were taken from selected acquisition reports (SARS) periodically prepared for submission to the Congress.

(21)   That the data actually were used cannot be proved; but they were available.

(22)   The underlying assumption here is of course that the program advocates, who, in securing program approvals also set program goals, consistently understate probable costs, overstate achievable performance, and underestimate development time.   Two important definitions: First, the "predicted program outcome" is that given for the "approved program" in the first selected acquisition report published after full-scale development began. The baseline used for comparisons ignores subsequent adjustments to those approved program projections. Second, the "actual" cost used in these calculations is a late 1977 cost adjusted for inflation and for any quantity changes.   The performance and schedule outcomes used for baseline comparisons are those actually reported to OSD by the services.

(23)   "System performance," as measured here, is actually a composite of many performance features called out in the individual program specifications.

(24)   In fact, the typical cost growth of the programs of the 1960s in the Rand sample was ultimately greater than 40 percent because some of the more costly programs experienced their greatest cost increases after the data sample had been evaluated.   A similar consideration may affect the 1970s sample, although no evidence of it was available by 1979 and the typical annual rate of cost growth was appreciably lower in the 1970s.

(25)   But for the prototyped systems of the 1970s (there were no prototypes in the 1960s sample), performance outcomes

were significantly better than for systems of the 1960s,
and schedule outcomes were modestly better.

(26) At least there is no record of it at Rand.

(27) Pre-1970 aircraft milestone data were adjusted to be
consistent with the definition adopted for DSARC II: the
start of a formal, finded, full-scale development effort.

(28) In some programs of the 1950s, prototypes were built as
an initial step in the development process. For such
cases, the start of prototype work was taken to represent the start of full-scale development. Although conservative, that premise seems realistic - for the 1950s.
In all cases, simple least-square trends were fitted to
the data.

(29) The F-18 was omitted because at the time the data were
normalized no 200th production article had been scheduled.

7 The Influence of the Civilian Sector on Military R & D
Alexander H. Flax

The U.S. has had a long tradition, not merely of civilian policy control of military affairs, which is mandated by the Constitution, but also of civilian involvement in the development and manufacture of military weapons. The latter aspect of military weapons acquisition goes back at least as far as the time when Eli Whitney obtained contracts for the mass production of muskets for the Army in 1798 in parallel with arsenal production by more traditional methods. But in the age of the scientific and technological revolution since World War I, the role of the civilian sector in the weapons acquisition process has taken on a much more pervasive character.

The military segment of the total U.S. industrial economy has never been large except in times of mobilization for war, and for this reason if for no other, the interaction of military R&D with civilian R&D has been of supreme importance in the U.S., the world's most industrialized nation. But the thesis of this chapter goes well beyond the mere mustering of civilian industry in direct support of military weapon systems programs, or even the consideration of the uses made of civilian-developed technology in military systems, although these can be important. Rather, it will be argued that military systems development in the U.S. and also abroad, on both sides of the Iron Curtain, is heavily influenced not only by civilian science and technology but also by civilian political, social, cultural, and economic factors whose impact is often not perceived or well understood. The issues relating to allocation of economic resources among industrial sectors will not be discussed here. There should, however, be no misunderstanding; there is a significant element of reciprocity in the relationship between the civilian and military sectors. For example, there is no denying that military technological

developments have had a profound effect on some areas of
civilian industry, especially in materials, aviation, and electronics. However, we will eschew here the simplistic notion
of a one-way flow (variously dubbed "spin-off," "fall-out," or
"trickle-down," depending on the bias or advocacy role of
protagonists for one policy or another).

Furthermore, although there have been many who have
maintained that in totalitarian countries, and especially in the
USSR, defense R&D is largely independent of the civilian sectors, the case will be made here that even in those countries
no such decoupling can be possible, particularly when factors
beyond direct technical and industrial support and interchange are taken into account.

OBJECTIVES, POLICY, AND PHILOSOPHY

All military establishments are created and maintained to
further national objectives and the strategy for attainment of
those objectives. Military R&D must serve the ends for which
these military establishments are created if it is to be valid
and effective. Increasingly, however, R&D is also being
undertaken by governments to meet other national objectives
even in areas which in many countries with relatively free
economies were formerly left largely to the private sector.
Underlying the rationale for national support of R&D in the
civilian sector and for substantial R&D funded by industry,
universities, and private foundations, has been the belief that
the social and economic well-being of the nation and its citizens can be improved by the advancement and application of
science and technology.

In the other advanced industrial societies, the emphasis
has been on closing the so-called technology gap with the
U.S, although, on examination, some of this concern appears
to have more to do with market factors and entrepreneurial
styles than with science and technology as such. Among our
closest allies this gap is felt to be most severe in a few advanced technology fields such as aviation, microelectronics,
instruments, and computers, and in France and Japan particularly, large well-funded efforts have been undertaken
over the past two decades to close the gaps with only modest
success thus far. (It should be noted that, as in the case of
Japan, a commanding market position over the U.S. in electronic devices and equipment can be attained without entirely
closing the technology gap in the most advanced microelectronics.)

The USSR has had as its state policy, claiming the
philosophical authority of Marxist-Leninist dialectical material-
ism, an all-encompassing belief in the need for scientific and

technical progress as a major requirement for the progress of society. Marx said that in the new society of the industrial state, the creation of both material and spiritual wealth would depend "on the general condition of science and on the degree of development of technology or on the application of this science to production."(1)   And repeatedly, in Soviet books and in speeches at Party congresses, one finds emphasis on the need to advance science and technology, and often a claim such as, "As in no other society, science under socialism and communism becomes a direct productive force, a vitally important area of social life."(2)

Thus we have in the East as in the West a readiness at the conceptual and policy-making levels to accept scientific and technical progress and a readiness to accept, indeed to seek, the changes which such progress brings about.   This attitude creates a general climate in which proposals for innovation in weapons systems, and for other high-technology machinery and equipment, can find relatively easy approval at the policy level.

Among the accepted reasons for national support of science and technology for military, economic, or social advantage, there is one which is possibly the most difficult to measure: the enhancement of national prestige.   Bailes recounts the Russian drive under Stalin before World War II to establish aviation records with specially designed and built aircraft.(3)   This was done even at the expense of the development of aviation necessary for defense.   There seems to be little doubt that the Soviet haste to bring the Tu-144 into operational service before the British-French Concorde, in spite of known technical difficulties which forced them initially to limit the aircraft to cargo operations only, was motivated by prestige.   This same thrust for prestige in seeking aviation records (which also in some vague way gives an image of military aviation prowess) has consistently led the almost fanatically secrecy-conscious Russians to reveal some of the performance of military aircraft thinly disguised by special designations (such as E-266 for the Foxbat) in record flights.

But the USSR and the U.S. have no monopoly on seeking prestige.   Sir George Edwards, one of the principal British managing engineers involved in the Concorde development, stated, in his Wilbur and Orville Wright Memorial Lecture before the Royal Aeronautical Society in 1973, that the great virtue of cooperative international programs is to be found in the political forces which keep them going.   For the Concorde, this was mainly the French using strong political pressure to keep the British government in it, but at times, in the course of the project, it was the other way around too.   It seems clear that prestige was a factor here.

ECONOMIC INFLUENCES ON TECHNOLOGY

The state of economic and industrial development of a nation may affect technological choices in many ways. The age of the capital plant in an industry, coupled with the rate of growth of capacity which the market can accommodate, will determine the receptivity of resource managers to introducing new technologies which require scrapping all or part of the existing plant and investing substantial sums in new plants. The classic recent example of this is the ease with which new production technologies in heavy industry were assimilated after World War II in Germany and Japan, which had suffered destruction of much of the older industrial plants - by contrast with the Western Allies, and especially the U.S., which retained most preexisting plants for many years after the war.

The relative costs and availability of the factors of production (labor, capital equipment, natural resources) will differ in different countries. Therefore, the "correct" technological solution to a given problem may vary from country to country. One country may choose to use labor-intensive systems and methods while another may choose capital-intensive systems and methods. In a comparison between British and American cost and technology in aircraft development and production, P. G. Hall of British Aerospace stated that, although British and American aircraft prices were generally competitive, the British man-hour productivity is only one-third that of the American.(4) Competitive prices with lower labor productivity have only been possible in the past because British salaries and certain other costs in the aerospace industry, such as reinvestments, have also averaged one-third as much per employee in comparison with American costs. The problem which arises now is the steady pressure for higher salaries in the face of inflation and the drive of British labor for a higher standard of living.

It is worth noting that if disparities in economic structure as large as those just described can exist in relatively mature industries with much common history and close contact, in two Western democracies as similar as the U.S. and Great Britain, the differences in similar economic variables in industry must in general be expected to be much larger and more widespread between the U.S. and the USSR. The extent and nature of such economic differences must vary in the various industrial sectors, and are certainly changing in time in the various industrial sectors - very rapidly in some sectors - in both countries. The process of change is driven not only by the internal pace of scientific and industrial development, but also by technology transfer, which is constantly taking place directly between the U.S. and the USSR

through licensing and technology exchange agreements as
well as through less visible third-country exchange mechanisms.

Given the variations in factor costs and availabilities already discussed, it must be recognized that, particularly in
totalitarian, centrally planned and controlled economies such
as the USSR, allocation of scarce and expensive factors of
production may be ordained by national policies to specific
objectives (for example, defense science, industrial development, energy) so that the "optimum" technologies may be different in the different sectors of the economy. However, not
every weapon component and subsystem technology can be
economically or even practically developed independently for
even the highest priority objectives.

Complete segregation of the military and civilian sectors
would impose a terrible economic burden on any nation which
attempted it. It seems safe to say that no modern nation
practices such general segregation by choice. Extremely critical or scarce materials, components, and devices may, of
course, be limited to high-priority uses, and some items may
be unique for one or a few applications; but in general, military and civilian sectors in every country draw on many
common sources in the economy.

CIVILIAN TECHNOLOGY FOR MAJOR
WEAPONS SYSTEMS

The capital-goods technology of evey nation has major interactions with military systems. Aviation and shipbuilding are
two major industries which clearly illustrate these interactions. But energy systems, communications systems, and the
machine tool and instrument industries are also of importance
in this respect.

In the U.S. before World War II, it is clear that the
high state of development of air-cooled aircraft engines relative to liquid-cooled engines could be attributed in considerable degree to the use of air-cooled engines but not liquid-
cooled engines in commercial transports. Military engine
development in the U.S. at that time depended to a considerable degree on industrial initiative, and it is not surprising
that this situation developed. On the other hand, the more
direct government control and funding in Britain of military
engine development no doubt contributed to their superior
position in liquid-cooled engines which found application in
many of the fighters of World War II.

In more recent times, there is no doubt that the great
impetus in both the U.S. and Britain, first for low-bypass
ratio turbofan engines and later for high-bypass turbofan

engines, came from their projected importance for air transport applications. Versions of low-bypass engines, first the
TF-30 and later the F-100 and the F-101, have powered virtually all new U.S. fighter-type aircraft for the past decade.
It is fair to assume that the apparent lag in Soviet development of turbofan engines is due in part to the lesser interest
and importance attached there to the need for air transports
with attractive operating economics (by Western standards).

The high-bypass ratio turbofan engine (TF-39) was first
developed for the C-5A transport. However, the two competitors for the C-5A engine were acutely aware of the commercial
transport possibilities for this class of engines from the beginning. It is interesting to note that, even today, the
Soviet Union appears to lack a suitable high-bypass ratio
turbofan engine for its wide-body jet transports.

What we have described here is neither a simple case of
military development benefitting commercial air transport nor,
on the other hand, a case of a simple purchase of commercially available technology from the marketplace to military equipment. Rather, it is a case of symbiotic nourishment of a
common pool of engine technology which serves both military
and civilian need, with each field of application not only
drawing on the pool but also constantly replenishing it from
field service results and evolutionary improvements made to
improve the performance, reliability, or maintainability of engines in operational transport and military vehicles.

The development of nuclear power plants for Navy sur-
face vessels and submarines has also had general technological
interchanges with the civil power-reactor program. Here the
naval reactor program has taken the lead in gaining operating
experience, and although the differences in system operating
environments is substantial, there is still a very useful contribution from the naval programs to civilian reactor technology.

Within the R&D and industrial organizations which produce the more complex capital goods such as aircraft, there is
the perennial problem of providing a relatively constant work
flow to maintain and support the highly skilled and tightly
integrated work forces that are necessary. Such work forces
cannot be easily laid off and reassembled. Hall describes this
as "one of the most difficult problems to solve or control"
because, if a project is successful, customers all seem to want
their aircraft delivered as soon as possible, and a peak production rate of early deliveries may then be followed by a
fall-off in which the fall of manpower requirements is exacer-
bated by the operation of the "learning curve."(5)

In the U.S. the aerospace industry went through a
painful reduction "from feast to famine" in the early 1970s,
after the 1960s orders for military aircraft to meet Vietnam
requirements, plus sales of a whole new generation of jet

transports for the world's airlines, compounded by the peaking-out of the manned spaceflight program, all combined to raise aerospace sales and employment to new highs. All of these markets for aerospace products either vanished for external reasons or were, at least temporarily, saturated by the early 1970s. Absent central, authoritarian government control of the aerospace industry, this could happen again.

In a centrally planned and controlled economy, the surrogate owners and high-level corporate managers of the development and production facilities required for high-technology industry are usually themselves in high government positions, often at or close to the ministerial levels and other policy-making and decision-making bodies. These manager-officials are charged with responsibility for efficient productive use of scarce human and capital plant resources. Their natural tendency would be to attempt to operate in accordance with a constant plant loading principle. Obviously, free rein cannot be given to this tendency in all economic sectors, but it may be an overall objective which is more strictly applied to some of the highest priority sectors, many of which will be military oriented.

This tendency to operate at constant levels may be evidenced, for example, in the almost steady rate of production of new models of Soviet ballistic missile systems for the past 12 years, thus keeping both design bureaus and production plants at approximately constant loading.(6) Except for a substantial growth and subsequent leveling off in helicopter output, total Soviet aircraft production for the past 12 years also shows a tendency to approximate a constant rate of output.(7) Indeed, the intelligence community characterizes this situation in the Soviet weapons-production infrastructure as the "no feast or famine syndrome" by comparison with the U.S.(8)

In the USSR the concepts of constant plant loading and "no feast or famine" appear to fit well with the mechanism for managing the centrally planned economy. If military R&D and production operate according to these rules, as the intelligence community seems to believe, it is not because they are special or different from the rest of the Russian economy, but, on the contrary, precisely because they are part and parcel of the Russian economy.

While most military R&D is, by nature, mission oriented, sometimes important new weapons potentials arise out of entirely new technologies, such as lasers, which have their origins in recent basic research for which both civil and military applications are clearly seen early in the transition to applications. In such cases, the military sector often takes the lead during the high-cost, high-risk part of the applications program. Then, when these initial barriers to more widespread applications are hurdled due to the "learning principle," both risk and cost come down, permitting large-volume civilian production and further "learning," which in turn benefits both civil and military applications. The operation of this "learning" feedback model is virtually independent of whether the original inventions or discoveries of the new science and technology took place in the military or civil sectors. The history of the development of the digital computer in the U.S. illustrates well the working of this model, and from what is available in the open literature concerning civilian and military digital computer development and production in the USSR, there is nothing that is inconsistent with the workings of this model there, too. There were no applications of digital computer technology in the Russian equipment observed in the October 1973 war, and there were none reported by the press in the Foxbat aircraft in which a defector escaped to Japan; in 1975, this state of affairs might have been expected, given the state of Soviet civilian computer technology in the late 1960s as described in both Western(9) and Soviet(10) writings. A most striking instance of the operation of the learning-feedback model was in the development and application of the integrated circuit, which will be discussed further in the section dealing with the consumer-goods sector.

An impressive example of how separate lines of technological development in military R&D can combine synergistically with civil development in both the capital goods and consumer goods areas is the case of the cruise missile. Cruise missiles are not new: the Navaho, the Snark, the Regulus, as well as Mace, Matador, and Hound Dog, which saw much operational service, date back 20 to 30 years. Yet, separate, seemingly unrelated advancements in a number of component technologies took place over this period which made possible, during the late 1960s, the synthesis of a new generation of cruise missiles so superior to their predecessors in respect to reduced weight, volume, and cost, and increased range, reliability, and capability to penetrate air defenses as to constitute virtually a new military capability. Perhaps the most important technological contribution to the modern strategic cruise missile, particularly in the guidance and control system, was the continuing development and application of solid-state microcircuitry which, although military contributions were not unimportant initially, depended for its current high-volume, low-cost maturity largely on the civil consumer goods sector. Modern microelectronics made it possible to have the required guidance-data storage and accuracy requirements met in a system packaged in a small, light, relatively cheap and reliable form. These guidance-system features contributed to keeping the cruise missile light, small, and of relatively low vulnerability to air defenses, and also aided in keeping system costs down.

THE ROLE OF CONSUMER GOODS TECHNOLOGY

Consumer goods span a great variety of products and services with highly diverse relationships to military equipment and supplies. Essential goods such as clothing, food products, shelter, and medical supplies carry over more or less directly to military use simply to serve the needs of human existence for the military and civilians. Nation by nation, these products often tend to fit the styles, tastes, customs, and practices of national, social, and ethnic groups, although these factors are almost always also shaped and modified by the level of economic affluence which has been achieved by such groups.

Thus, there is an inevitable tendency for the quality and style of civilian life to follow the soldier into the armed forces from his previous civilian incarnation. Standards of health care and sanitation in the armed forces may be better than those of some economically underprivileged groups in the civilian society, but these standards generally tend to move up with the norms of society as a whole, and although such upward movement may make a positive contribution to military effectiveness, it is usually not that factor which is the driving force for continuing upgrading of the standards.

Similarly, practices in manufactured goods which affect human safety, comfort, and convenience are likely to be carried over into military equipment. Thus, if U.S. automobile drivers and tractor drivers are accustomed to commodious, air-conditioned, power-steered vehicles, similar amenities are likely to be found on military trucks and tanks. If such amenities are rare or nonexistent on Soviet automobiles and tractors, they are much less likely to be provided on Soviet military vehicles.

Another area where civilian standards seem to apply to military systems is in that of living space and environment. Living space in new dwellings for Soviet citizens is planned at about 90 square feet per person(11) while corresponding U.S. figures are three to four times this. Also, comparative studies of U.S. and Soviet naval vessel design show that U.S. space allowances per man on ships for such purposes as berthing, medical services, sanitation, food preparation, messing, stores, administration, and recreation are almost twice as great as on Soviet ships. Space and machinery allowances for such amenities as air-conditioning, laundries, and dry cleaning are also considerably less on Russian ships.(12)

Thus, it is apparent that as the affluence of a society increases and the creature comforts and quality of life of its citizens improve, there is, in effect, a social cost imposed on military installation, structures, equipments, systems, and modes of operation because of the tendency to carry civilian amenities into all walks of military life.

Consumer-goods technology also contributes importantly to military equipment and weapons systems and interacts synergistically with military technology in much the same way as discussed for capital-goods technology. The integrated-circuit technology is perhaps the outstanding recent example. Here, although in the 1950s there was a high level of military support for semiconductor R&D in general and for several concepts of microminiaturization of electronic circuits in particular, the invention of the integrated circuit did not occur in a military-sponsored R&D program.(13)

However, the existence of a high level of military interest in microminiaturization of electronics, and the existence of a market in which the first relatively high-cost integrated circuits could be sold, were undoubtedly strong motivating factors in inducing or accelerating commercial initiatives. ("Sales" to DOD also involved R&D support for pilot production and manufacturing techniques development as well as essential contributions to a body of technology relating to applications of integrated circuits.) In 1963, 100 percent of all production of monolithic integrated circuits went to the DOD (for Minuteman II guidance system application); by 1972, the DOD share of production had dropped to 15 percent. Over the same period, the average price of such circuits had dropped from 50 dollars to 1 dollar. The high-quantity production for the consumer market (such as calculators and watches) had brought down the price, improved quality and performance, and made available a variety of types, thus greatly expanding the range of applications for integrated circuits from only very high value components and equipment to the entire range of military electronics.

The growing conversion of virtually all civilian electronics in the U.S. to solid-state components and integrated circuits has rapidly outmoded all older electronic technologies. The rapid pace of change in electronics poses many problems in military equipment and systems which in the past have been procured and maintained based on life cycles of 20 years and more. The problem for the military is one of acquiring (at high cost) replacement parts such as vacuum tubes, which are not only no longer in general production, but are manufactured by methods and processes no longer in general use. The issue for the military is not whether the older technology is adequate (or perhaps even "better"), but rather how to assure logistic and maintenance support of systems without creating an industrial base completely independent of civilian production.

Soviet military electronics equipment, as seen after the 1973 Middle East War in the Foxbat which a defector flew to Japan in 1976, still made extensive use of older vacuum-tube

technology. This, however, corresponds with the technology
of their radio and TV sets. In some "real" economic sense,
labor costs for production and maintenance of such equipment
must conform to the prevailing price structure of the Soviet
economy (administered though it may be).

Although, as we have shown, there are very strong interactions between civilian and military technologies, it is
important not to assume either the universality of such interactions or the automatic functioning of interchange mechanisms
independent of political forces. It should be recalled that
prior to World War II, when there was hardly a refrigerator
or similar major electrical appliance to be found in a British
middle-class home, the British fighter planes and British
radar were second to none in the world.

LITTLE TECHNOLOGY - BIG TECHNOLOGY

The World War II Manhattan Project which led to the development of nuclear weapons was the archetype of modern "Big
Technology." (This is more often called "Big Science," but
surely the bigness was more associated with technology than
with science, if a distinction be made between science and
technology.) All of the subsequent R&D on nuclear weapons
has been carried out under institutional arrangements much
like those of the Manhattan Project: a few large government-sponsored and controlled "national" laboratories and
development organizations monopolized the entire field. Since
the government itself had a total monopoly on nuclear weapons
from their conception through their entire life cycle, and was
strongly motivated to prevent at all costs the diffusion,
transfer, or dissemination of the technology of weapons design and manufacture, a "Big Technology" approach to
nuclear weapons R&D was natural.

The development of microwave radar in the U.S. during
World War II was also highly centralized in the Radiation
Laboratory of MIT, but with much more latitude for industrial
participation, especially in the hardware aspects. But this
was in no sense a monopoly. The military laboratories and
their industrial contractors had been involved in VHF radar
R&D long before the "Rad Lab" came into existence. The institutional centralization of radar R&D did not survive the
war, and although the MIT Lincoln Laboratory has some degree of consanguinity to the "Rad Lab" and has, among other
things, made several interesting and valuable contributions to
radar technology, in no sense does it have a central role in
the radar R&D.

By contrast with nuclear weapons and radar, the jet engine - the third military technological wonder to reach opera-

tional status during World War II - was basically a product of
"Little Technology." The development was, both in Germany
and Britain, the work of individual inventors (von Ohain and
Whittle, respectively) working initially through large-scale
laboratory model or prototype demonstrations outside the aircraft powerplant industry and without government support.(14) After some degree of success had been achieved,
government support and the participation of the aircraft engine industry came, and was probably essential to the quantity production of operational engines. However, without the
initiative of private inventors working against the initial
skepticism of both government and industry, jet-engine development would not have taken place when it did.

Even when not centralized in one or a few institutions,
massive government-sponsored programs aimed at major advances in technology often tend to narrow rather than
broaden the options for progress. An example was the drive,
in the late 1950s, by the three military services to micro-
miniaturize electronics.(15) As it turned out, the next success in microminiaturization, and one which has proved to
retain its dominance for decades, was along a line not contemplated in any of the service programs. This was the integrated circuit, initially developed in private industry without direct government funding - although, as already noted,
the incentives of an identified government market and government funding for applications and R&D certainly played an
important role in bringing integrated circuits to early
maturity.

The Soviet system most often tends to emphasize "Big
Technology" rather than "Little Technology," at least in
public statements of the political leadership and in institutional responses to new scientific and technological opportunities and initiatives. Typically, the Soviet approach is to
establish large, well-funded programs with extensive experimental facilities and often expensive, large, pilot plants
and prototypes. Magnetohydrodynamic electric power generation is an example of a technological development in which the
USSR committed itself early to a large-scale operational 25
megawatt prototype. In the U.S., on the other hand, critical
component technologies were explored by industry and the
electric utilities, and several unsolved high-risk problems
were discovered which inhibited proceedings to larger-scale
R&D.

Given that R&D is always a gamble, particularly in the
more speculative advanced technologies, hedging more bets
will result in at least some successes which a more cautious
and conservative approach would never realize. The Soviet
achievements in MHD power generation cannot yet be counted
a success in terms of commercial applications; nor does it
appear that the program has achieved major technical "break-

throughs" in critical MHD technologies. Yet the program
continues to be pursued aggressively,(16) and it cannot be
said that success in a practical and commercial sense will
never come. In the field of nuclear fusion power, in which
the USSR has had a greater degree of technical success than
the U.S. (in achieving an intermediate goal), it is at least
possible that the Russian achievements with the Tocamuk
prototype reactor were as much a result of their boldly
charging ahead with an aggressive large-scale prototype effort as it was a consequence of their shrewder insights into
the mechanics of plasma processes.

A centrally planned and controlled R&D program can ac-
comodate large-scale efforts concentrated in one or a few organizations much more readily than it can deal with a proliferation of small efforts by scattered individuals and groups of
inventors and researchers. Moreover, perhaps not surprisingly, Soviet writings on increasing the effectiveness and efficiency of "scientific production" stress bigness. There is
no reason to doubt that the Soviet "Big Technology" approach
to projects assigned high national importance, urgency, and
priority applies equally well to military and civilian technology. Analysts of Soviet writings relating to military-technological affairs(17) have argued, in fact, that the apparent
greater degree of efficiency and success of Soviet military
R&D over civil R&D is attributable to a "Manhattan Project"
syndrome in defense R&D programs, referring here to a
readiness to resort to extraordinary management procedures
to overcome all barriers. Such unusual procedures from on
high can best be administered by concentration of programs.

Clearly, there are some R&D programs for which a "Big
Technology" approach may be almost essential, and others in
which it may be counterproductive. The most comprehensive
of recent studies of the origins of technological innovation(18)
lead to the conclusion that there is no royal road to innovation either through "Big Technology" or "Little Technology,"
but rather that progress should be allowed to occur in whatever diverse ways a variety of institutions and individuals
may choose, leaving them to find financial support from whatever sources, public or private, may be available.

Yet scientists and engineers are conditioned by their
own experiences, and many in the U.S. whose direct, first-
hand involvement in military R&D has been in the nuclear
weapons programs or the Radiation Laboratory during World
War II, are quick to suggest the "national" laboratory solution
in any major new problem, from command, control, and communications to precision-guided weapons. They tend to for-
get that (1) there is no government monopoly in these technical areas and that closely related civilian technologies exist
and are developing rapidly in many places throughout the
private sector, and (2) absent a war and the mobilization of

manpower and resources which occurred during World War II, the forces which made it possible to muster large concentrations of talent and competence into one or a few "national" laboratories are not operative in a democratic society and a relatively free economy.

For the most part, the Defense Department in the U.S. has generally avoided overcentralization of its R&D institutions, although the pressures for economy, avoidance of unnecessary duplication, and "efficient" management have certainly been at work, especially in the past 20 years, and have resulted in multilevel review and approval processes in the R&D program and funding processes. The forces at work in the Soviet society and economy are quite different, and their concentration of specific areas of R&D activity into rather large organizational units tends to be commonplace both in the military and civilian sectors.

THE STRUGGLE BETWEEN SIMPLICITY AND SOPHISTICATION IN THE UNITED STATES

It is common in some quarters to accuse the military R&D establishment (or the military-industrial complex, as the case may be) of needlessly and wastefully adding technical complexity and cost to new weapon systems, perhaps not consciously and willfully, but as captives of their own misbegotten military requirements and R&D planning and management systems. Sometimes this does happen, but need, waste, and cost are subjective notions charged with bias, bias conditioned by value judgments, emotions, and sincerely held conviction. Moreover, the civilian scientific and technological environment in which the military establishment operates plays a much larger role in driving the rate and direction of change in military equipment than is usually thought.

From the last years of the Eisenhower administration to the Nixon administration, the White House scientific advisory apparatus (comprising the president's Scientific Advisory Committee, the Office of Science and Technology, and the various panels operating under their standards) stood at the pinnacle of outside scientific influence on government programs, including military programs. When the F-111A program got underway, the Air Force, recognizing potential for technical risk and cost growth in the implementation of important new concepts in both airframe and engine (for example, the first operational aircraft to have variable sweep wings, and the first operational aircraft to have variable sweep wings and the first operational afterburning fan engine), decided not to attempt a great leap forward in avionics, but rather to use "state of the art" avionics. However, more ambitious avionics were then coming into existence. An advisory panel under White House auspices shortly came forth with a condemnation of the obsolescent and inadequate F-111A avionics, and strongly recommended that the fruits of modern avionics technology be exploited to achieve a much higher level of military capability. Their recommendation was seconded by the Air Force's own Scientific Advisory Board, also composed of civilians from the academic and industrial communities. As a result, the Air Force R&D community working with industry came forward with a proposal for the Mark II avionics package for the F-111.

Debate within the Air Force was mixed, with many strong voices, both civilian and military, against introducing such complications in the already complicated F-111 program. The matter was finally decided by Secretary McNamara, who directed that the MK II avionics go forward.

The incremental cost of the MK II avionics, including RDT&E and nonrecurring cost for 97 units, was contracted for at $145 million. By the time the program had reached the production stage, numerous technical difficulties and costly schedule delays had been encountered, and the putative cost, including overrun reports and claims from several tiers of contractors, had reached a figure over $800 million. Even excluding nonrecurring costs, the cost of avionics per aircraft was then estimated at over $4 million, some three times as great as original estimates.

The role of the civilian scientific community here was to draw attention to the immense possibilities of the electronics revolution, already well on the way to the modern integrated-circuit components we now take for granted, and to press for military applications. Whether this pressure was wise or premature will not be argued here; too much of the argument would hinge on assessments of Air Force and DOD procurement and management practices and whether they were properly and effectively applied to the acquisition program for the F-111 Mark II avionics. But the outcome was clearly a case in which the better was the enemy of the good. (It should be noted that the Air Force was at the same time employing integrated-circuit technology in the Minuteman II guidance system(19) where cost-reliability-performance trade-offs and overall technical risk factors were much more favorable to the nascent technology of integrated circuits.)

The White House science advisory apparatus, at about the same time, also put forth a strong case for the widespread adoption of V/STOL aircraft by the military across a wide mission spectrum. This view was strongly resisted by the DOD, which argued that V/STOL aircraft was an immature technology which, except for its unique landing and takeoff characteristics, suffered from degradation in performance and greater costs in relation to more conventional military charac-

teristics. The DOD view prevailed, and it was only later that
a more mature V/STOL design, the British Harrier, was
adopted by any U.S. military component. By the time this
occurred, pressure from the civilian scientific community was
not a significant factor in bringing about the decision.
Rather, it was the military requirements process, so often
maligned by the U.S. civilian community, which found in the
newly developed Harrier a seemingly most apt solution to
Marine Corps amphibious landing problems.

But there is no intent here to suggest that the civilian,
scientific, and technical advisors always opted for the most
advanced high-performance systems just because they embodied the latest and best in technology. The White House
scientific advisory apparatus also included severe critics of
the B-70 supersonic high-altitude strategic bomber program
and the C-5A long-range Navy military transport. The B-70
opposition was not based on questions of technical feasibility,
a fact which nonplussed many of the uniformed military, but
of military need and military utility, based on an understanding of the problems of penetrating modern air defenses
at high altitude, and on a knowledge of the potential capabilities of alternative strategic systems, mainly missiles. The
C-5A opposition from the civilian scientific community was
based on no technical factors at all, but rather on operational
and economic factors.

A particular U.S. military weapon system debate in
which the civilian scientific and technical community clearly
drove the decision toward a novel but relatively (and "relatively" must be stressed here) less comlex, less sophisticated,
and less costly system than other alternatives was in the case
of the cruise missile. Most of the proximate driving force
which led to the decision for full-scale development and deployment came from civilians in the Office of the Secretary of
Defense, although there was a background of advocacy and
support from outsiders, particularly in the early stages of
advanced development.

SIMPLICITY VERSUS COMPLEXITY IN
SOVIET WEAPON SYSTEMS

On the Soviet side, we really have little knowledge of the
forces currently at work for and against simplicity in weapon
systems. With particular reference to the role of the civilian
scientific community in influencing decisions on Soviet military
R&D, it is clear that Soviet civilian scientists and scientific
institutions, especially the USSR Academy of Sciences, have
been and are involved in conducting and contributing to
military research programs, particularly in fields involving

newer sciences or new technological applications of science.
However, as Holloway has pointed out, this involvement appears to have been less important in sectors where an institutional R&D base was long established, such as in aviation
and shipbuilding.(20)

Thus, the civilian scientists and engineers play important roles in the execution of some military R&D programs
in the USSR. In these roles, they undoubtedly influence
military R&D by bringing up for consideration new technical
advances for military application, by participating in choosing
the specific technological approaches to be used in the development of new military systems, and by making forecasts of
feasibility, technical risk, and the potential for technical advance to assist planners.

But when the issues revolve about what should be developed rather than what can be developed or how can it be
developed, the role of the civilian scientific community becomes more obscure. Even the part played by the Soviet
state science-policy agencies in managing military R&D is not
obvious and may be largely in meeting the needs of the
defense sector in a service role.(21)

We know that during World War II and into the 1950s
many of the Soviet systems, especially aircraft, were somewhat simpler than ours, although our aircraft of that era
were also very much simpler than they are today. But the
extent to which this has been a free choice or simply the
result of factors quite beyond the control of Soviet designers
and decision makers (for example, limitations of their technology and industrial base) is by no means so clear. Much of
our knowledge is ancient and anecdotal. The much-quoted
work by the noted Soviet aircraft designer, A. S. Yakovlev,(22) contains a number of references to the virtues of
simplicity in aircraft design in the period before and during
World War II. (The frequent reference to this book in the
literature on Soviet technology no doubt stems from the lack
of much similar recent writing by military systems technologists.) Yakovlev's work becomes less and less specific
about the design considerations and operational experience as
he discusses military aircraft subsequent to 1960. But U.S.
analysts using unclassified materials must work with what is
available, and are led to conclusions accordingly. For example, Gallagher and Spielman conclude that "an overwhelming
impression emerges from Yakovlev's book which points to a
certain built-in constraint in that scientist's attitude toward
innovation...namely, the cautionary impact of wartime experience."(23)

Yet Yakovlev himself points to the three stages of the
Soviet plan to "catch-up" with the rest in transitioning to
jet-powered aircraft, in which "measures outlined by the government determined the rate at which engine construction

proceeded in the Soviet Union."(24)   The first two stages as
he describes them were indeed slow and cautious.   The first
stage consisted of installing captured German jet engines in
aircraft kept as nearly as possible like their piston-powered
predecessors.   The second stage was based on the use of the
British Derwent and Nene engines (whose thrust levels and
specific fuel consumptions distinctly limited the size, weight,
and equipment installations and allowances of aircraft employing them).   It should be noted, however, that within
these constraints very respectable and competitive Soviet aircraft, such as the MIG-15 fighter and the IL-28 light bomber,
were produced.

The third stage of Soviet jet-aircraft development was to
be based on Soviet designed and built jet engines, permitting
for the frst time a degree of flexibility comparable to that
enjoyed in the West in tailoring engines to aircraft configura-
tions and military concepts.   The products of this third phase
were first displayed to the world at the Tushino air show in
1961.   Yakovlev says that these were "superfast, super-long
range with a superhigh ceiling" and that they "were equipped
with exceedingly good instruments, enabling them to fly
throughout the year in any weather and to reach their target
accurately."(25)

Finally, it must be noted that, in his account of the
state of Soviet aircraft technology after 50 years of the Soviet
state, he says, "A characteristic feature of the Soviet school
of aircraft construction is its firm theoretical foundation,
bold-design thinking infused with a spirit of constant innovation, the development of ideas with long-range view in
mind of scientific and technical progress in aviation and fields
connected with it."(26)   Although it may be tempting to dis-
miss this as mere nationalistic, jingoistic propaganda, or to
try to prove that the innate caution, conservatism, and
reverence for simplicity in design have always overridden the
urge for innovation in Soviet aircraft and weapon systems,
this would be a position very difficult to sustain in light of
what we now know concerning Soviet weapon systems since
1961, especially since the Domodedovo air show in 1969 and
the information on Soviet ground-force weapon systems which
surfaced during the October 1973 war in the Middle East.
The BMP armored personnel carrier, the ZSU-24-4 radar-
directed mobile anti-aircraft gun system, and the SA-6 mobile
ground-to-air missile system and related command and control
equipment are all, though well-designed and effective, examples of complexity rather than simplicity, the more so because of the minature vacuum tube electronics components and
the analogue computer subsystems the Soviets employed in
them.

Thus, it may be said that in the Soviet Union, as in the
U.S., increasing sophistication, complexity, and cost have

come to characterize the prevailing trend in weapon systems. And, although the corresponding situations in the weapon systems of our major industrial allies, Britain, France, and West Germany, have not been included in this discussion, there is ample evidence that this same trend is being followed in those countries as well. Only cost seems to be at all effective as a limiting factor, and unfortunately, in the case of the Soviet Union, we know little of this factor in the design of weapon systems.

Paradoxically, in the West, operating costs, especially manpower costs, seem likely to increase rather than to decrease the trend toward technological sophistication and complexity of a weapon, as greater effectiveness is sought from fewer, more expensive weapons, requiring ostensibly relatively less manpower for operation, maintenance, and support over their life cycles than a larger number of simpler, cheaper, less-effective weapons. The cost of manpower and direct support in the West is almost entirely driven by conditions in the civil economy, and military equipment and force structures are necessarily as influenced by economic factor costs in the civil economy in the large as well as by the availability of civilian advanced technology in specific civil sectors important to weapon-systems design.

Studies of the contemporary Soviet civil economy(27) emphasize that constraints and inhibitors against innovation are built into the system of Soviet industry. This is said to be because the prime measure of management success is fulfillment of production plans and goals over relatively short periods of time. Any change or innovation involves risk of at least temporary disruption of production with little, if any, reward for success. In fact, improved quality of new and better products is reported to be not usually taken properly into account in setting new production plans, goals, and norms, and if innovation increases productivity, norms are merely raised, resulting in no lasting benefit to the innovators. The absence of market forces and the inflexibility and artificiality of the administered price system are listed among the principal causes of the disincentives to improve products or production processes. Yet, at the policy level, there is constant exhortation to accelerate the improvement of both the quality and quantity of production through innovation. For example, in 1971 Brezhnev said, "it is necessary...to create conditions to compel enterprises to produce the latest product innovations, to literally chase after scientific-technical novelties.... Collectives which truly fight for improved machinery and technology...must be given the most privileged positions.(28)

Conversely, the ability of authoritarian societies to decide on, centrally plan, and execute major national programs of great urgency, ruthlessly commandeering the neces-

sary human and material resources, is often cited as one of
their strengths.

In Western societies not all significant technological
progress takes place in sectors in which the free play of
competitive market forces and highly elastic prices are to be
found. The government sector is the principal instigator of
innovation and the principal, if not the only, customer for
the products in the areas of military equipment, nuclear
weapons, space vehicles, and, in many countries, communications systems. In these areas, it may be argued that even in
the Western industrial democracies, the benefits of private-
sector economic forces, to the extent they can be enjoyed,
depend on a spill-over of entrepreneurial and management
style and practices and profit motivations prevailing in industry and in the society at large. However, it would seem
that many of the real advantages which contribute to the advancement of technology in Western societies arise from factors such as the diversity of technical and industrial organizations, institutions, and practitioners comprising sources of
ideas, techniques, instruments, machines, equipment, and
components quite free of rigid centralized controls.

CONCLUSIONS

Civilian society, economy, and industry, as well as science
and technology, play major roles in influencing the development, production, and deployment of military equipment and
systems. In every nation, the standard of living and life
styles in society have a significant influence on requirements
and specifications for military installations, equipment, and
systems affecting the acquisition and logistic support of both
material and personnel. An affluent society thus exacts a
social tax on its military establishment. The wage scales of
civilian society inevitably influence the costs of military
equipment, and new civilian technologies, bringing both
higher average standards of living and higher wages, may
price older and perhaps "better" (handcrafted) technologies
out of the realm of affordability in both the civilian and military spheres. The rapid rate of obsolescence of some technologies, such as electronics, in the highly developed nations
drives the development of new military systems development
and force-modernization in the West at a certain rate in order
to contain the costs of maintenance and support.

Civilian technology in both the capital-goods and
consumer-goods sectors also interacts with military technology, both by providing new innovations and by feedback of
the "learning" process in design, production, and utilization,
even for innovations initiated or first utilized by the military.

This "learning" process frequently results in cost reduction which broadens the range of military applications of new technologies (for example, integrated circuits).

Although the consumer-goods sector is much more resistant to change in centrally planned and controlled economies such as the Soviet Union, as contrasted with the freer economies of the industrial democracies, the differences are not nearly so marked in the capital-goods sector - for example, in aviation, shipbuilding, communications, and energy generation and conversion.

The pursuit of international prestige as an instrument of political influence, real or imagined, also plays an important part in providing strong support for certain fields of science and technology, which have high interest and visibility on an international scale. This has been evidenced in the evolution of many civilian space programs, the race between the French-British Concorde and the Russian Tu-114 for the first start of supersonic air transport operations, and the heavy stress laid on high-energy particle accelerators and large radio telescopes at various times in both the U.S. and the USSR. These prestige projects both draw on and contribute to many technologies of potential or demonstrated military importance.

The centrally planned and controlled economies are generally considered to lack the incentives for innovation that are found in economies which are more responsive to market forces. As noted, this distinction applies more to the consumer-goods sectors of civilian economies than to the capital-goods sectors. Direct extrapolation to national-prestige R&D projects and to military R&D projects is not at all obvious.

The nations in which all R&D is centrally controlled and planned seem almost to require concentration of priority R&D areas into "national" laboratories and similar institutions, whereas in the industrialized democracies the R&D activities, even in high-priority areas, tend to be more widely spread among many and various performing organizations. This latter diversity tends to enhance the possibility of novelty and innovation not contemplated in government programs, as exemplified in the inventions of the jet engine and integrated circuits. On the other hand, organizations of the "national" laboratory type, with stability of program and funding and assured continuity of staff, may be better adapted to rapid exploitation of technology to projects of very large scale and to developing existing technologies toward major well-defined objectives, especially in the civilian capital-goods sector, in the military sector, and in national-prestige projects. The organizational stability in programs, funding, and staff tends to drive output of "national" laboratories and development organizations in centrally planned and controlled economies (as well as associated manufacturing organizations) toward a constant rate of output in new projects, systems, or major modifications of systems.

Underlying the major national commitments to the advancement of science and technology and to innovation as an important process in the economy, there must be the philosophical and ideological basis as well as the constituencies and institutions to energize the political system. These requirements are met in both the industrialized democracies and the industrialized communist countries. In the democracies, in spite of some zero-growth advocacy in recent years, it has been an article of faith since the days of Jefferson and Hamilton that science and technology, whether in agriculture, civilian industry, or for national defense, were to be vigorously pursued to better the condition of the nation and its citizens. In communist countries, the dialectic-materialist philosophies espoused by Marx, Engels, and Lenin are cited in support not only of the importance of technological advance but also to assert that only in communist societies can the full potential of modern science and technology be realized.

The higher levels of the political hierarchy in the developed communist countries are the prime advocates of science and technology and of innovation in all sectors of industry and economy. They are aided and abetted by the scientific, technical, and military communities in important ways, although the detailed workings of the interactions among these groups are not well enough known to assess the relative importance of the different groups in various areas of R&D.

In the developed democracies, and particularly in the U.S., the diffusion of political authority leaves the role of advocacy to individuals both in the legislative and executive branches, usually on a more or less program- or agency-specific basis. The U.S. civilian scientific and technical community plays a much more visible and probably more important role as program advocates or critics and as an elite political constituency for advancing science and technology than do similar groups either in communist countries or in the other Western democracies. In particular, the formal scientific advisory apparatus serving the executive branch, and the usually less formal channels of advice to the legislative branch, have had important influences on major programs, both military and civilian. With or without such advice, the interplay between the executive and legislative branches has had a profound effect on both civilian and military R&D, and significant advocacy for or resistance to a program or system in either branch can have important effects on the rate and direction of progress on that program or system.

The Soviet R&D system, with its inexorable buildup of momentum in programs once started, can, if carried to the extreme, certainly lead to much inefficiency and waste. The

U.S. system of increasing checks, balances, and delays at all stages of the military R&D process may, on the other hand, lead to paralysis and inadequacy if carried to the extreme. The trends and tendencies in both countries will bear careful watching in the next few years.

NOTES

(1) V. G. Afanasyev, The Scientific and Technological Revolution: Its Impact on Management and Education, translated by R. Daglish (Moscow: Progress Publishers, 1975),
p. 80.
(2) Ibid., p. 80.
(3) K. E. Bailes, Technology and Society Under Lenin and
Stalin (Princeton: Princeton University Press, 1978), pp.
381-406.
(4) P. G. Hall, "The Simple Arithmetic and Hard Facts of
Our Survival and Standard of Living," The Aeronautical
Journal 82, no. 815 (November 1978): 457-466.
(5) Ibid.
(6) "Allocation of Resources in the Soviet Union and China:
1978, Part 4 - Soviet Union," Hearings, Subcommittee on
Priorities and Economy in Government of the Joint Economic Committee of the U.S. Congress. (Washington,
D.C.: U.S. Government Printing Office, 1978), p. 229.
(7) Ibid., p. 227.
(8) Ibid., p. 223.
(9) R. W. Judy, "The Case of Computer Technology, " in
S. Wasowski, ed., East-West Trade and the Technology
Gap (New York: Praeger, 1970), pp. 43-72.
(10) Colonel Y. M. Bodarenko, "Scientific-Technical Progress
and Troop Control," in Selected Soviet Military Writings,
1970-75, translated and published by U.S. Air Force
(Washington, D.C.: U.S. Government Printing Office).
(11) L. I. Brezhnev, Main Address to 24th Party Congress,
March 30, 1971, FBIS.
(12) J. W. Kehoe, Jr., "Warship Design: Ours and Theirs,"
U.S. Naval Institute Proceedings, August 1975, pp.
56-65.
(13) N. J. Asher and L. D. Strom, "The Role of the Department of Defense in the Development of Integrated
Circuits," IDA Paper, P-1271, May 1977.
(14) R. Schlaifer and S. D. Heron, Development of Aircraft
Engines and Fuels (Boston: Graduate School of Business
Administration, Harvard University, 1950), pp. 332-348,
377-392.
(15) H. S. Kleiman, "The Integrated Circuit: A Case Study
of Product Innovation in the Electronics Industry,"
Ph.D. dissertation, George Washington University, 1966.

(16) V. Latyshev, "Power Source of the Future," Soviet Life, No. 9 (252), September 1977, pp. 12-17.

(17) M. P. Gallagher and K. F. Spielman, Soviet Decision Making for Defense (New York: Praeger, 1972), p. 70.

(18) J. Jewkes, D. Sawyers, and R. Stillerman, The Sources of Invention, 2nd ed. (New York: W. W. Norton, 1969), pp. 184-186.

(19) J. S. Kilby, "Invention of the Integrated Circuit," IEEE Transactions on Electron Devices, July 1976.

(20) D. Holloway, "Soviet Military R&D: Managing the Re-search Production Cycle," in J. R. Thomas and U. M. Kruse-Vaucienne, eds., Soviet Science and Technology: Domestic and Foreign Perspectives (Washington, D.C.: George Washington University Press for NSF, 1977), p. 201.

(21) Ibid., p. 215.

(22) A. S. Yakovlev, Fifty Years of Soviet Aircraft Con-struction. Translated from Russian by E. Vilim (pub-lished for NASA by the Israel Program for Scientific Translations, 1970).

(23) Gallagher and Spielman, Soviet Decision Making for Defense, p. 99.

(24) Yakovlev, Fifty Years of Soviet Aircraft Construction, p. 103.

(25) Ibid., p. 106.

(26) Ibid., p. 159.

(27) A. Nove, The Soviet Economic System (London: Allen and Unwin, 1977), pp. 163-164.

(28) Brezhnev, Main Address to 24th Party Congress.

8 The Soviet Style of Military R & D*
David Holloway

The Soviet Union and the United States mount the two largest
military R&D efforts in the world: no other country comes
near them in the scale of military R&D or the range and
sophistication of the equipment they develop. It is only in
recent years that attempts have been made to analyze Soviet
military R&D in the open literature, and it is still the case
that, by comparison with the research on U.S. weapons
acquisition or on Soviet civilian R&D, our knowledge of it is
small.(1)   Yet the topic is so clearly important, not only for
an   understanding   of   Soviet   policy   but   also   from   the
perspective of arms control and its possibilities, that it seems
worthwhile to pursue its study, in spite of the difficulties of
obtaining information.   In this chapter I shall look at the
characteristics of Soviet weapons, the size of the military R&D
effort, the structure of the weapons acquisition process, the
driving forces of military R&D, and at current problems and
trends.

SOVIET MILITARY TECHNOLOGY

The Soviet Union is undoubtedly a formidable military power,
but this power cannot be taken as direct evidence of the level
of military technology. A distinction has to be drawn between

*Much of the work for this chapter was done in July-August,
1978 when I was a Visiting Fellow at the Peace Studies
Program, Cornell University. I am grateful to F. A. Long,
Judith Reppy and Milton Leitenberg for stimulus and ideas,
and to the Rockefeller Foundation for funding my visit.

the effectiveness of a weapons system and the level of technology embodied in its component parts. It is, within limits, possible to design, on the basis of a lower level of technology, a weapon which is superior from the military point of view to one which incorporates more advanced technology. In other words, design is the process whereby the whole can be made greater than the sum of its parts, and thus enters into the relationship between technology and military effectiveness. At a more general level, the relationship between the quantity and quality of weapons affects the military value of a force: a superior force can be created from equipment which is inferior in quality if that equipment is available in larger quantities or is organized or used more effectively. These are obvious points, but need to be borne in mind if one is to avoid jumping from the evident military power of the Soviet Union to conclusions about the level of technology.

It is commonly assumed that in the Soviet Union the level of military technology is higher than that of civilian technology. The studies available do bear out this assumption, but they do not show that there is a qualitative difference between the two; some areas of Soviet civilian technology are highly developed. A study of Soviet technology from the early 1950s to the early 1970s has concluded that the Soviet Union did not close the technological gap with the West, and even fell further behind in some advanced areas; but there are traditional areas - such as the iron and steel industry or high-voltage electric power transmission - where the Soviet Union has remained among the world leaders.(2) Given that there is an interrelationship between civilian and military R&D, it is hard to see how the levels of the two realms could be completely divergent, unless one assumed that two wholly separate R&D networks existed in the Soviet Union. The available studies show that the level of military technology in the Soviet Union - when measured in terms of the comparative dates of major innovations and their diffusion through stocks of weapons - is lower than in the United States; in other words, the Soviet Union has not been the progenitor of major military-technological innovations.(3) It is true that the Soviet Union has created some types of equipment which the United States does not possess and some weapons which have characteristics that American weapons do not have, but this has been a matter of choice and not of technological capability.

There are those who argue, however, that it is choice and not the level of technology that is the important issue, and that the Soviet Union has a way with technology that enables it to extract the maximum military value from its R&D, while the United States squanders its technological power in an ineffective and wasteful manner. This argument usually points to "nontechnological" factors in explanation of this alleged difference. One of these factors is the level of effort, which will be discussed in the next section. In recent writings on Soviet military R&D particular emphasis has been laid on design philosophy and on the relationship between doctrine and technology.(4) The Soviet Union, it has been argued, has a design philosophy of evolutionary development, commonality, and simplicity which enables it to extract more military value from its R&D. There are two difficulties with this argument. One is that, while these elements are present in Soviet weapons development, they are also to be found in U.S. military R&D. It may be that the Soviet Union exhibits these characteristics to a greater degree, but it is wrong to lay too much stress on this design philosophy as a distinctive feature of Soviet weapons development. A sharp contrast cannot be drawn across the whole range of weaponry between a Soviet practice of evolutionary development and an American predilection for revolutionary innovation.(5) The other difficulty is that while the concept of "commonality" is clear, those of "simplicity" and "evolutionary development" are not: "simplicity" can embrace the different senses of "crude" and "elegant," while "evolutionary development" can be interpreted very strictly to mean incremental product improvement or rather loosely to cover everything short of major discontinuous change (for example, the application of atomic energy to military power).

Secondly, it is frequently stated that in the Soviet Union military doctrine determines technology; in other words, military requirements are derived from doctrine and these requirements determine what weapons are developed and procured.(6) The corollary of this is that Soviet weapons are exactly tailored to Soviet military purposes and serve those purposes well. This too is a misleading description of the weapon acquisition process, for it ignores the fact that Soviet military doctrine has undergone major revisions in response to postwar technological change, and it overlooks the influence of the arrangements for R&D on the design, development, and production of weapons. Moreover, the relationship between doctrine and technology may vary from one kind of innovation to another.

THE SIZE OF THE SOVIET MILITARY R&D EFFORT

Since 1929 the Soviet Union has given very high priority to the development of its defense industry and to the creation of modern armaments. Starting from a very weak base, this policy achieved considerable success in the 1930s and produced large quantities of weapons, some of which were of a very high quality (for example, the T-34 tank and the Il-2

Shturmovik). Constrained by the low level of technical skills
of workers and troops, designers sought to create designs
that were easy to produce and would stand up to rugged use.
If the quality of the equipment was sometimes lower than that
of its foreign counterparts, then this could be compensated
for by producing it in large quantities. The Soviet Union
also engaged in "advanced" R&D (for example, in rocketry
and radar); but apart from the Katyusha rocket artillery,
these programs yielded no results for the war with Germany.

The war proved the value of the Soviet policy and reinforced the lesson that what was important were designs that
were easy and cheap to produce in mass quantities. The war
also showed, however, that major revolutions were taking
place in military technology and that the Soviet Union, not
least because of the ferocity of its struggle with Germany,
lagged in important new areas of weaponry. By the end of
the war Stalin had taken steps to make good this lag, and
with help from German technology, launched major R&D programs in radar, jet aircraft, rocketry, and nuclear weapons.
The results of these programs became evident in the 1950s
and caused (to use a Soviet term) a "revolution in military
affairs." It became increasingly clear that technological innovation was a crucial element in military power and that the
Soviet Union (in particular because access to foreign military
technology was much more difficult than in the 1930s and
1940s) would have to make a major R&D effort if it was not to
fall behind its more advanced rivals.

Just what resources are devoted to military R&D is extremely difficult to say. The output of the military R&D effort can be seen in the new and improved equipment that is
developed, but the inputs to the effort are a closely guarded
secret. The first problem is to estimate total R&D outlays,
but even here there are difficulties in deciding precisely what
the Soviet figures cover. Moreover, even when estimates are
made, it is difficult to compare Soviet and foreign efforts.
What, for example, is the appropriate exchange rate between
an R&D dollar and an R&D ruble (or even trickier, between
a military R&D dollar and a military R&D ruble)?

Further problems arise in establishing the proportion of
total effort devoted to military R&D. Estimates here range
from 40 to 80 percent. The most careful Western study
(which has serious, if unavoidable, methodological weaknesses) suggests that military R&D absorbed between 40 and
60 percent of Soviet "science" expenditures (or a rather lower
proportion of an expanded definition of R&D outlays) between
1960 and 1968, with the military share showing a tendency to
decline in that period.(7) The higher Western estimates -
those where the methodology is open to inspection - prove all
too often to be derived from assumptions that build in the
proportion at the very beginning of the exercise.(8)

It follows from this that estimates of Soviet military R&D outlays are extremely unreliable as indicators of the size of effort. We know that the effort is large from the equipment it turns out, but it is impossible to work back from this to an assessment of the inputs because it is difficult to say how efficient the R&D process is (and such figures would not provide independent evidence of the size of the effort). It may be presumed that the resources devoted to military R&D have grown more or less in line with total "science" expenditures (from which the bulk of military R&D appears to be financed), although it is possible that the military proportion has declined as civilian R&D has become more important. The CIA estimates that between 1967 and 1977 Soviet military R&D accounted for 20 to 25 percent of defense spending, and was equal to 40 to 50 percent of investment outlays. In the U.S. these proportions are about half: 10 to 12 percent of the total military budget and 25 to 30 percent of the funds available for acquisition.(9) Even with the Soviet stress on science and technology, this seems a very high proportion to sustain over such a long period, although the contrast may be explicable in part by differences in the activities covered (the CIA's figures are derived largely from Soviet statistics and are acknowledged to be the least reliable part of its estimate of Soviet defense spending). Perhaps all one can say is that the Soviet military R&D effort is large and has continued to grow in line with rising total R&D outlays, absorbing a proportion of that total that is more likely to be 50 percent than 25 or 75 percent.

STRUCTURE OF THE WEAPONS ACQUISITION PROCESS

The two main elements in the weapons-acquisition process are the defense industry ministries which design, develop, and produce equipment, and the Ministry of Defense, which places orders, supervises development and production, conducts acceptance trails, and assimilates the final products. The Politbureau is the most authoritative policy-making body in weapons acquisition, as in other areas, and it directs and supervises the activities of both these elements. Control is exercised through the Defense Council, which consists of top party and military leaders, and the Military-Industrial Commission, which is an executive or implementing agency, as well as through the central party and state apparatus. (See Fig. 8.1.).

There are now nine ministries in the defense industry group. These engage primarily, but not exclusively, in military production, and are organized in the same way as other industrial ministries in the Soviet Union, although they

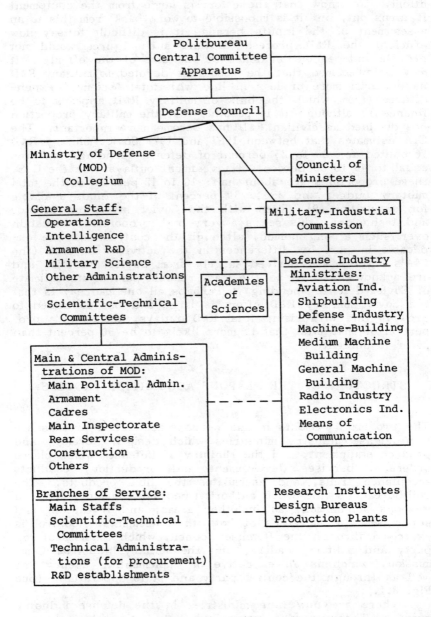

Fig. 8.1. Organizations in USSR Military R&D.

have some special features of their own. The most important
of these features is the high priority that defense production
has received for fifty years in the allocation of resources and
in the arrangements for planning and administration.   This
priority gives the defense sector first call on scarce materials
and skilled manpower, and enables it to commandeer resources
from civilian industry.   The defense industry ministries are
characterised by a high degree of vertical integration.   Because of their high priority, they have been able to create
their own supply industries; but the necessity for doing this
shows that high priority is not effective in ensuring that the
needs of the defense sector are readily met by the civilian
economy.(10)

      Not all production under these ministries is for defense
purposes; in 1971, 42 percent of their output was civilian
(for example, civil aircraft, merchant ships, consumer goods;
the Ministry of General Machine-Building, which develops and
produces strategic missiles, is the chief ministry for samovar
production).(11)   Military equipment is also produced by the
plants of ministries not in this group; indeed, a large proportion of Soviet industry appears to have some military
production.   The civil-military distinction is becoming less
sharp as a result of changing technologies and of new practices in the management of R&D.

      Like other industrial ministries in the Soviet Union, each
of the defense industry ministries controls production plants,
where weapons, subsystems, and components are produced;
research institutes, which engage in applied research both in
weapons and production technology; and design bureaus
which design and develop weapons and major subsystems, as
well as production technology.   The research institutes and
design bureaus are administered by a technical adminstration
which is responsible for overall R&D policy in the ministry.
A scientific-technical council, which includes the ministry's
leading scientists, engineers, administrators, and perhaps
consultants from outside (for example, from the Academy of
Sciences), advises the minister on R&D policy.

      From the point of view of military R&D, the important
institutions are the research institutes and the design bureaus.   The former are often large, well-equipped organizations, with a considerable reputation and directed by leading
scientists - for example, the Central Aerohydrodynamics Institute (TsAGI) of the Ministry of the Aviation Industry.
Applied research in the relevant areas is concentrated in such
institutes.   The design bureaus, like the institutes, specialize
in either weapons or production technology.   In some cases,
especially in such traditional areas as artillery and armor, the
bureaus are attached to series production plants.   In other
fields, notably aerospace, they are independent organizations
with factories of their own for producing prototypes; then

they are called experimental-design bureaus (OKBs). In very advanced or new areas of technology the research institutes and design bureaus may be joined together in one organization with production facilities of its own. The pattern of organization is thus not uniform throughout the defense sector.

In spite of this lack of uniformity, it is possible to point to some general features of the standard operating procedure of R&D in the defense sector. First, applied research is by and large institutionally separate from design and development. The funding of applied research does not appear to depend directly on specific orders of equipment, although it will depend in a more general way on the importance which a particular area is seen to have for weapons development. Similarly, military production seems not to be as subject to fluctuations as in the U.S., so that the design bureau is supported by a steady applied-research effort, and in turn serves a steady rate of military production. Second, the role of the designer is crucial, for it is his task to try to match foreign weapons while working from a lower technological base. The importance of the chief designers is underlined by the fame which they have enjoyed (for example, Yakovlev, Mikoyan, Tupolev, Korolev, Kalashnikov). The work of the designers is constrained in a number of ways: by design procedures which the research institutes lay down in handbooks; by the norms which the ministry sets for the use of scarce materials and the control which it exercises over their allocation; and by the Ministry of Defense, which has representatives in the bureaus to see that the requirements which have been agreed upon are adhered to. These constraints will encourage standardized design procedures.

Third, the designer, when faced with a new requirement, is likely to try to meet it with what is at hand (although that may, of course, not prove possible). There are various reasons for this. It may be too troublesome to try to remove the constraints that are imposed by other agencies. Because supply problems are chronic in the Soviet economy (even if less severe in the defense sector), a design which depends on completion of a new or difficult order by another ministry will expose itself to the risk of failure. In this way commonality in the use of subsystems and components will be encouraged. The designer may well be innovative in his use of existing technologies (for example, in applying cold launch in ICBMs), but he is unlikely to want to push for major innovation in component technologies, unless absolutely necessary. The separation of applied research from development suggests that the designer will turn to the research institute and take what is available, rather than wait for something new; because development programs are not the way in which funds are acquired for applied research, there is no incentive to go for fancy designs. These factors help to explain the practice of getting a design into production and then modifying it as new components and subsystems become available (hence the proliferation of different models). They might also be thought to encourage conservatism and evolutionary development; however, if a large applied research effort is under way, it may provide the basis for major intergenerational changes in design and technology.

Fourth, competition between design bureaus has been a common, though by no means universal, practice in weapons development. Two or more design bureaus may be given the same requirements and asked to produce designs; the Ministry of Defense then selects the best design for development. This gives the customer a degree of choice unusual in the Soviet economy. In a limited number of cases competition may extend in the development of prototypes, with the choice made only after weapons trials. In some instances weapons that appear to be competitive developments have gone into production. It may be, however, that the redundancy here is more apparent than real, and that the weapons designs either started with different missions or acquired new missions during the acquisition process.

It may be objected, in the light of this, that Soviet weapons must be characterized by evolutionary development, commonality, and simplicity. This might indeed be the case if the characteristics of Soviet weapons were determined only by the standard operating procedure of the R&D establishments. But other factors intervene to upset this pattern, and these will be examined in the next section. Here I shall turn to look at the role of the Ministry of Defense in military R&D, since it is this institution that acts (to use the expression of one Soviet article) as "legislator" in procurement policy.

The role of the Ministry of Defense in military R&D is to issue requirements, request design proposals, agree on development contracts with the design bureaus, supervise development, conduct prototype trials, place orders for production, supervise production, and assimilate new equipment. The Ministry possesses the institutional arrangements and the technical competence to perform these tasks. The General Staff has a scientific-technical committee which helps to devise R&D policy, and this presumably calls on outside advice and expertise to help identify promising lines of R&D and to check proposals put forward by the designers or the branches of the armed forces. Since 1947 there has been a deputy minister of defense either for armament or electronics (from 1964 to 1970, a deputy chief of the General Staff) with responsibility for supervising development and production programs. Since 1978 there appear to be two such deputy ministers, one each for armament and electronics.

At a lower level, the five branches of the Armed Forces have technical administrations which deal directly with their suppliers, issuing requirements, conducting tests, and sending representatives to the design bureaus and production plants. The branches also have scientific-technical committees to advise on R&D. The armed forces should, therefore, have a good knowledge of what is going on in Soviet science and technology; moreover, the Ministry has an Institute of Military-Technical Information which disseminates information to staffs, technical administrations, academies, and research establishments, and this presumably covers foreign developments.(12)

The technical administrations work closely with the appropriate staffs, which are responsible for force planning, doctrine, and combat training. Each branch of the armed forces has R&D establishments whose work is mainly related to the role of the armed forces in weapons acquisition: their task is to help the armed forces decide on their operational requirements, to monitor foreign developments, and to test and employ new equipment.(13) These establishments may engage in some weapons development, but most of this is done in the design bureaus of the defense industries. The military academies also play an important part in military R&D: the Zhukovskii Air Force Engineering Academy and the Malinovskii Academy of Armored Forces, for example, have done considerable work on operational analysis and weapons design. No class of civilian defense analysts has grown up in the Soviet Union: analysis is done in military institutions.

The basic document which regulates weapons development is the Tactical-Technical Instruction (TTZ: taktiko-tekhnicheskoe zadanie) which is prepared by the technical administration and agreed to by the design bureau.(14) This sets out the purpose of the development; the tactical-technical and technical-economic requirements (that is, the operational and cost specifications) of the prototype; the composition and stages of preparation of the technical documentation. The TTZ is used by the technical administration as the basis for monitoring development work. When a prototype or model is prepared it will undergo factory trials and then go for state trials, which determine how the system will perform under operational conditions; these latter trials are conducted by the armed forces.

If the design is approved for series production, a document called the technical conditions (TU: tekhnicheskie usloviya) is prepared which sets out the purpose of the product, the basic tactical-technical data, the parameters that govern its suitability for delivery to the customer, the methods of quality control, and so on. This is in effect a contract between the technical administration and the production enterprise, and forms the basis for the quality control exercised by the military representatives at the plant. The military representatives at a large plant will consist of military engineers, technicians, and office personnel, and will be headed by a "field grade officer equal in experience and status to the plant manager."(15) They exercise quality control throughout the production process and conduct tests to ensure that the equipment delivered to the armed forces meets the standards laid down in the TU. They also have the right to supervise the calculation of production costs, and apparently try to exclude all indirect costs from such calculations.

It is generally true of the Soviet economy that vertical links (such as between enterprise and ministry) dominate horizontal ties (such as between enterprise and enterprise). This is true of military R&D too. The technical administrations will be closely directed by the General Staff and the deputy minister of defense for armament, while the design bureaus are subordinate to their own ministries. Every large development or production program will have to go to the Ministry of Defense Collegium and the Defense Council for approval, and to the Military-Industrial Commission to see if the necessary resources are available. All new types of production in the Ministry of General Machine-Building, for example, are regulated by special decrees of the Council of Ministers.(16) These ratify the contracts between the Ministry of Defense and the design bureau. In practice the decrees are probably drawn up by the Military-Industrial Commission and issued in the name of the Council of Ministers. Further, it is not clear whether the Ministry of Defense itself disposes of funds for R&D; it can probably finance small-scale work, but is likely to require approval from some higher body for any major commitment of funds. However, it does appear that contract work is becoming more important in the defense industry's R&D establishments (hitherto financed exclusively from the budget), and this may give the Ministry of Defense greater flexibility in placing orders with those establishments.

The role of the Armed Forces in weapons acquisition seems to reinforce the tendency toward evolutionary development: the complex committee structure for approving new development programs is likely to inhibit innovation, while the different elements of the armed forces might be expected to press for follow-on systems - pressure that will be welcome to the design bureaus, since it will keep them occupied with designs that are not too challenging.

Figure 8.2 provides a schematic diagram of the Soviet weapons-acquisition process. There is one major actor which does not fall into the defense industry or the armed forces: the academies of sciences (the most important being the USSR Academy and its Siberian Division, and the Ukrainian Acad-

RESEARCH ———→ REQUIREMENTS ———→ DESIGN & DEVELOPMENT

AGENCIES

Research institutes of defense industry ministries; Academy institute; MOD establishments.

Most important are the branch research institutes which do research on component technologies; the Academy institutes which do basic research and work on very advanced technologies; and the MOD's in-house establishments which keep the armed forces abreast of scientific and technological developments.

AGENCIES

Branches and arms of service; technical administrations of MOD; General Staff; MOD Collegium; MIC; Defense Council

The requirement for a new system will probably be initiated by the branch or arm of service that will use the weapon. It will have to be approved at a higher level - by the General Staff or the MOD Collegium. Large projects will go to the MIC and the Defense Council. The requirement is formalized as document - the TTZ - by the technical administration after negotiation with the design bureau.

AGENCIES

Design bureaus of the defense industry; technical administrations of MOD

Designs may be prepared by one or more design bureaus, perhaps before the TTX is finally formulated. The bureau - or more - will proceed to development. The design bureau works under constraints imposed by the branch research institutes (on design procedures), the Ministry (allocation of materials), the MOD (through its military representatives). The bureau often has production facilities; prototypes may be produced and undergo factory trials.

Fig. 8.2. Schematic diagram of acquisition process.

PRODUCTION DECISION ⟶ PRODUCTION

AGENCIES

Design bureaus; technical
administrations of MOD;
General staff; MOD Colle-
gium; MIC; Defense Council

State trials of prototype
will be conducted under
military supervision. De-
cision to produce will be
taken on basis of trials
(which may be competi-
tive), in context of overall
plans for the armed forces.
Production decision (in-
cluding numbers to pro-
duce) will have to be taken
by bodies with a broad
military and economic re-
sponsibility; such as MIC,
MOD Collegium, Defense
Council. Contract, in
form of TU, is concluded
between MOD and supplier
(design bureau).

AGENCIES

MIC: defense industry plants;
design bureaus; military representatives

Production is organized by the
ministry (perhaps by the MIC
for large programs). In some
cases production plants come
under the control of the design
bureau. The TU document
serves as basis for quality control by military representatives
from the technical administration.

Abbreviations:

MOD – Ministry of Defense;
MIC – Military-Industrial Commission;
TTZ – Tactical-Technical Instruction;
TU – Technical Conditions

Fig. 8.2 (continued)

emy). Academy institutes played a crucial role in military R&D in the 1940s and 1950s. In the early 1960s the Academy was reformed to concentrate on basic research, and many institutes (including the Kurchatov Institute of Atomic Energy and the Institute of Radio Engineering and Electronics) were transferred to the industrial ministries. The Academy still does applied research in very advanced technologies, some of which (for example, control systems, lasers, and charged-particle beams) have military relevance. When Academy institutes become involved in military R&D programs it is probable that they, or the relevant parts, pass under the control of the Military-Industrial Commission.

Two features of Soviet military R&D should be noted here. The first is that the philosophy and practice of design and development vary from one field to another, depending in part on the research intensity of the field. Two quotations will make the point. The first was made in 1974 by a man who had worked in the Tank Industry Commissariat during the war:

> The experience of the war shows that the design process ensures rapid introduction into series production only when it is based on assemblies which have been mastered earlier. Consequently, the continuous improvement of the basic assemblies is essential. To design a new tank, while at the same time creating new assemblies, means, as a rule, passing on for series production an uncompleted tank.(17)

The second was made in 1963 by Lt. Gen. V. Pyshnov of the Engineering-Technical Service:

> The fact is that a new military aircraft is not set within the framework of well-established technical capabilities, but always represents a major step forward and is developed with means which have been recently tested or have not been checked at all.(18)

In other words, in high-technology areas the use of existing tried-and-tested subsystems might be desirable, but may just not be possible.

In tank development a self-conscious philosophy of evolutionary development has been created as a result of wartime experience and the influence of Soviet military doctrine, with its stress on the shock power of massed armor. Here the emphasis on quantity has remained strong, and a clear pattern of evolutionary development can be discerned - as it can in Western tank development. In ICBM development, on the other hand, evolutionary development - in the sense of

incremental product improvement - has not been a dominant
feature of design and development. There are clear differences between the individual missiles deployed (although
many of the ICBMs have been deployed in several modified
forms) and, more important, between the different generations. Great stress has been laid on the quality of the missiles, and a large research effort has been aimed at their improvement. This effort has provided the basis for major
technological advances from one generation to the next. What
one does find, however, is institutional continuity in the design bureaus (for example, the GDL-OKB has provided the
liquid-propellant motors for all long-range missiles so powered
since 1948(19)), and strong evidence of a "follow-on imperative"; but it would be wrong to confuse this with evolutionary
development narrowly defined.

Further, even within the same general area of weapons
development, different designers have espoused different
philosophies. In aircraft development, for example, Yakovlev, whose comments on design have served as the basis for a
great deal of generalization about Soviet weapons, stressed
simplicity and the use of available technology. Myasishchev,
on the other hand, was known for his ambitious and innovative approach.(20) It is true that Myasishchev lost his
design bureau in the 1940s and again in the late 1950s, and
that this shows the dangers of being too innovative in the
Soviet system (though his fate had much to do with changing
attitudes to long-range bombers). But Myasishchev's case
should alert us to the dangers of generalizing too freely
about Soviet design philosophy.

The second feature is that weapons development is not
the product of military requirements or military doctrine
alone, although these clearly play an important role. The
history of Soviet military doctrine in the postwar years has
been dominated by adjustment to new military technologies:
the major turning-points in the development of doctrine -
1954, 1960, and 1967 - are all associated with changing views
about nuclear weapons and their impact on the conduct of
war. Moreover, there is an obvious sense in which the armed
forces have to formulate their requirements in the light of
technological possibilities and productive capacity, and hence
negotiate them with the R&D establishments and the defense
industry. As General Pyshnov remarks, the customer cannot
given the designer "figures at will."(21)

Furthermore, the pattern of innovation and deployment is
strongly influenced by the way in which the design bureaus
operate. In tank procurement there is a good fit between the
stress on quantity in military doctrine and the capacity of the
tank industry to turn out large numbers. In the ICBM program the structure of the force is strongly influenced by the
existence of several design bureaus which specialize in dif-

ferent types of missile and engage in partial competition with
one another. More generally, the arrangements within the
defense sector - between research institutes, design bureaus
and production plants - have an important influence on the
style of Soviet military R&D, and these arrangements are a
product not of military doctrine but of the Soviet system of
economic planning and administration.

THE DRIVING FORCES OF MILITARY R&D

The Soviet Union has been engaged, both before and after
World War II, in military rivalry with powers that are technologically more advanced. In the late 1920s, the Soviet
leaders espoused the goal of "catching-up and overtaking" the
advanced capitalist world, both economically and technologically, and this has remained an important objective for the
post-Stalin leadership. The Soviet leaders have not been
reconciled to backwardness in technology, whether civilian or
military. They have given high priority to the creation of
military power and have established mechanisms to extract
resources from the economy and the society to meet what they
have seen as the needs of international competition.
    The Soviet Union soon found that its rivals were not
content to stand still, and aircraft designs that seemed advanced in the early 1930s proved in the Spanish Civil War to
have fallen behind advances made elsewhere in Europe in the
1930s. In the immediate postwar years Stalin organized
special programs to make good the lags in military technology,
but once again the Soviet Union found itself in competition
with a main rival that was technologically more advanced and
more innovative - and one that had, moreover, the objective
of maintaining superiority in military technology.
    From this it follows that international competition has
been a major driving force in Soviet military R&D and has
provided the justification for a large effort. In a more specific way, too, one can point to new paths of weapons development that have been stimulated by foreign technological innovations - whether in emulation (atomic bomb development)
or as a counter to foreign systems (air defense and ABM
systems). In some cases the requirements generated by this
competition have pushed Soviet designers to develop systems
that have been technologically overambitious. Two examples
here are the SS-6 ICBM which, although it passed its state
trials in 1957, was unsatisfactory as a military missile (it was
not until 1962 that the Soviet Union had truly operational
ICBMs), and the Galosh ABM system which, although deployed, is thought to be quite ineffective. Similar examples
of systems that were overambitious in terms of existing tech-

nology were the Mya-4 (Bison) long-range bomber and the
first M(I)RVs which were not successful enough to be deployed in any numbers. Perhaps the attempt to develop
charged-particle beam weapons falls into the same category.
A civilian example is the Tu-144 SST.

The point here is not to decry Soviet technological capabilities, but rather to stress that none of these systems fits
the pattern of evolutionary development or confirms that the
Soviet designers always go for systems that are well within
the state of the art. These examples also suggest that the
needs of international military rivalry - as these are defined
by the Soviet leaders - have provided a major impetus to
technological innovation.

It is true, of course, that the way in which the requirements of international military rivalry are defined is very
strongly influenced by political, historical, geographical,
doctrinal, and bureaucratic factors which fall outside the
scope of this paper. Consequently, the interaction between
Soviet and foreign (especially U.S.) military R&D is complex
and cannot be reduced to a simple stimulus-response model.
Further, it cannot be assumed a priori that just because the
United States has driven Soviet military R&D, the reverse is
not also true. It is conceivable that a technologically backward state will drive the military R&D of a more advanced
state if the latter has a doctrine of technological quality (that
is, superiority) which is designed to offset the former's advantage in the quantity of men and arms. Some elements of
this kind of relationship have existed in the U.S.-Soviet arms
race, although it is not possible to explore them here.

There is a second driving force in Soviet military R&D
which is provided by a very large research effort in fundamental and applied science. As has been seen, designers
can draw on this in seeking to meet the requirements laid
down by the political leadership or the armed forces. This
research effort (along with foreign scientific research) also
provides scientific and technological discoveries which scientists or designers may want to exploit for weapons development. For example, A.P. Aleksandrov proposed the development of nuclear propulsion units for ships, Tupolev pressed
for the development of a nuclear-powered aircraft, and V. P.
Glushko investigated the possibility of nuclear-powered rocket
engines. Thus, designers are not always conservative in
what they propose if they see the opportunity for a technological breakthrough.

Major innovation decisions cannot easily be accommodated
within the standard operating procedure of the military R&D
system, and require intervention from the top to authorize
new funding and new institutional arrangements. The literature on Stalin and Khrushchev shows that they intervened
often in the weapons-acquisition process to set up new pro-

grams or to change the direction of existing ones. The same kind of evidence does not exist for the Brezhnev period, but there is little doubt that a similar flexibility exists, even if the style of decision making is different. Brezhnev was Central Committee secretary with responsibility for heavy industry, including the defense industry, in the late 1950s, and D. F. Ustinov, the present minister of defense, who was a Central Committee secretary from 1966 to 1976, has been a leading manager of weapons development and production since before the war. He is likely to have considerable power in military R&D policy. The political leadership can draw on various bodies - the Military-Industrial Commission and the Central Committee's Defense Industry Department, for example - and on individual scientists for advice and expertise that are not limited to particular industrial or military interests.

The two main driving forces of Soviet military R&D are international military competition, which exerts both general and specific pressures, and a large research effort which provides the basis for the development of new and improved weapons. Both of these forces act in a complex way on weapons acquisition. If the military R&D effort is rooted historically in international rivalry and strongly influenced by that rivalry, it is also true that the large military effort has created institutions which occupy a powerful position in the Soviet system and provide a dynamic of their own to military R&D. But the guiding force in Soviet military R&D has been the exercise of authority by the party leaders to devote resources to the creation of military power and to initiate major development and procurement programs.

CONCLUSION

Three conclusions about Soviet innovativeness are suggested by this chapter. First, the military R&D arrangements are well suited to the development of follow-on systems where no great shift in mission or technology is required. In such cases the R&D system ensures that user requirements are well understood in the development process; here we may indeed say that weapons development responds to military requirements. The cumulative military effect of such development may of course be considerable.

Second, the Soviet Union has been able to organize Manhattan-Project-style innovation when the leaders have deemed it necessary. The Soviet system is well suited to the concentration of resources on specific goals, although past history suggests that the selection of such goals may be a complex and hazardous process - in particular because of the scarcity of resources. This suggests that if the United States enjoys a lead in a major new weapons technology (MIRVs, cruise missiles) the Soviet Union will try to close the gap by concentrating its effort on that area.(22) Such programs may ultimately lead to major changes in military institutions and military doctrine.

Third, the Soviet system is not well adapted to the lateral or horizontal transfer of technology across departmental boundaries, unless this is organized as a matter of priority from the top. Low-level cross-fertilization between different branches of technology appears not to be encouraged by the Soviet system. The reasons for this lie in the compartmentalization of Soviet industry, and especially of the defense sector where this rigidity is reinforced by secrecy. It is difficult to say how important this defect is, or how far it is overcome by military management of the acquisition process. But Western studies indicate that ease of communication and movement of people and ideas are important factors in innovation, and these are lacking in Soviet military R&D.

Soviet military R&D is sometimes pointed to by Western commentators as worthy of emulation, not merely in its supposed size, but also in its style. It is worth noting, therefore, that Soviet writers do express anxieties about the operation of their military R&D. First, there has been anxiety about the costs of the R&D effort, and this has shown itself since the early 1960s in more open discussion of the need for cost-effectiveness, and an awareness of rising intergenerational costs. Second, Khrushchev's fall was followed by expressions of concern about the way in which R&D decisions were made. The military press underlined the need for "scientific" policymaking in which the professionally competent - that is, the military - would have a greater say. This argument reflects real concern about the complexity of R&D decisions, and an extensive literature has grown up about operational analysis and weapons selection. Finally, concern has been expressed about the flexibility of the R&D system; in effect, this is anxiety about innovativeness, for the argument here is that new technological opportunities are not exploited quickly enough and that new ideas are translated too slowly into production.

These arguments have accompanied a growing military R&D effort, a greater military voice in policymaking (even if the final decisions remain with the political leadership), and some attempts to improve the working of military R&D. But I see no evidence that these concerns portend a major overhaul of the system. It is true that it is not as innovative as might be desired, but it has been very effective in helping to create a powerful Soviet Union. Besides, it is flexible enough to accommodate high- and low-technology systems, as well as some differences in design approach. The present trend of reform in the Soviet Union is to transfer certain features of military R&D to the civilian sector, and this suggests that, whatever its shortcomings, the military R&D effort is regarded as successful and worthy of imitation. This is likely to continue until and unless a major reordering of priorities or reorganization of the whole R&D system is undertaken by the political leadership.

NOTES

(1) See, for example, Arthur J. Alexander, R&D in Soviet Aviation, R-589-PR (Santa Monica, Cal.: Rand Corporation, 1970); Armor Development in the Soviet Union and the United States, R-1860-NA (Santa Monica, Cal.: Rand Corporation, 1976); Decision-making in Soviet Weapons Procurement (Santa Monica, Cal.: Rand Corporation, 1978); Adelphi Paper Nos. 147-8 (London: International Institute for Strategic Studies, 1979); D. Holloway, "Technology and Political Decision in Soviet Armaments Policy," Journal of Peace Research, no. 4 (1974); D. Holloway, "Soviet Military R&D: Managing the 'Research-Production Cycle'," in J. Thomas and U. Kruse-Vaucienne, Soviet Science and Technology (Washington, D.C.: George Washington University for NSF, 1977); D. Holloway, "Military Technology," in R. Amann, J. Cooper, R. W. Davies, eds., The Technological Level of Soviet Industry (New Haven: Yale University Press, 1977). I have not provided extensive references for this chapter. The detailed evidence can be found in two chapters in R. Amann and J. Cooper, eds., Innovation in Soviet Industry (forthcoming).

(2) Amann, Cooper, Davies, eds., The Technological Level of Soviet Industry.

(3) Ibid. See also the evidence given by the CIA in Joint Economic Committee, U.S. Congress, Allocation of Resources in the Soviet Union and China - 1977. Hearings before the Subcommittee on Priorities and Economy in Government (Washington, D.C.: U.S. Government Printing Office, 1978).

(4) In particular by Colonel Richard G. Head, "Technology and the Military Balance," Foreign Affairs, April 1978.

(5) See the reply to Head's article, by Alexander Flax, Foreign Affairs, Fall 1978, pp. 207-211.

(6) Head, "Technology and the Military Balance," p. 548.

(7) N. Nimitz, The Structure of Soviet Outlays on R&D in 1960 and 1968, R-1207-DDRE, (Santa Monica, Cal.: Rand Corporation, 1974).

(8)   For example, the claim made by John Foster, DDR&E, in 1971 that 80 percent of Soviet R&D outlays were going to military purposes.   See General Accounting Office Staff Study,   Comparison of Military R&D Expenditures of the United States and the Soviet Union. Part II.   Declassified Version, DOD Methodology for Assessing United States and Soviet Union Military R&D Efforts   (Washington, D.C.:   U.S. Government Printing Office, January 1972).

(9)   CIA: Estimated Soviet Defense Spending: Trends and Prospects, SR 78-10121, June 1978, p. 3.

(10) In the mid-1970s, the Electronics Industry had to produce hundreds of components and materials it needed because it could not rely on outside suppliers (that is, other ministries) to meet their quality requirements.   P. M. Stukolov, ed., Ekonomika elektronnoi promyshlennosti (Moscow: 1976), pp. 14-15.

(11) L. I. Brezhnev at the 24th Party Congress, Materialy XXIV s"yezda KPSS (Moscow: 1971), p. 46.

(12) Voennaya Mysl', 1966, no. 9, CIA FD FPD 0558/67, p. 9.

(13) See V. M. Bondarenko, Sovremennaya nauka i voennoe delo (Moscow: 1976), pp. 41-42.

(14) Sovetskaya Voennaya Entsiklopedia, 3 (Moscow: 1977): 616-617.

(15) A. Sheren, in Joint Economic Committee, U.S. Congress,   Economic Performance and the Military Burden in the Soviet Union (Washington, D.C.:   U.S. Government Printing Office, 1970), p. 126.

(16) M. Agursky, The Research Institute of Machine-Building Technology, The Hebrew University of Jerusalem, The Soviet and East European Research Centre, Soviet Institutions Series Paper No. 8, Sept. 1976, p. 34.

(17) I. V. Yurasov, in P. N. Pospelov, ed., Sovetskii Tyl v velokoi Otechestvennoi voine. Kniga II. Trudovoi Podvig Naroda (Moscow: 1974), p. 113.

(18) In Voennaya Mysl', 1963, no. 10, CIA FDD trans. no. 10, p. 6.

(19) V. P. Glushko, Development of Rocketry and Space Technology in the USSR (Moscow: 1973), p. 20.

(20) G. Ozerov, Tupolevskaya Sharaga (Frankfurt am Main: 1973), pp. 48-60.

(21) Ibid., p. 6.

(22) Ustinov commented that "those who count on attaining military superiority over the Soviet Union with the help of such weapons [new types of weapons of mass destruction] should remember that the economy, science and technology in our country are now at such a high level that we are in a position to create in the shortest time any type of weapons on which the enemies of peace might wish to count." Kommunist, 1977, no. 3, p. 18.

V
Political Control of Military R & D

9 Organization and Process in Military R & D
Edwin A. Deagle, Jr.

In fiscal year 1980 the Carter administration proposes to spend $13.5 billion for military research, development, tests, and evaluation - about 10 percent of the entire defense budget and about 2 percent of the overall federal budget.(1) For the remainder of 1980 the disposition of the administration's plans will be hotly contested in Congress, as was the design of its plan in the executive branch in the fall and winter of 1979; so it has been in the past, and so it is likely to be in the future. As anyone who has walked the halls of the Pentagon knows, the struggle for control over military research and development (R&D) was joined in the aftermath of World War II and has continued unabated with quiet ferocity to this day. In part this is so simply because military budgets are always at the center in the competition for public resources, and consequently military R&D will be too.

But the argument advanced here is that, for several reasons, control over the military R&D process is a uniquely complex and sensitive issue deeply embedded in decisions about the structure and capabilities of the armed forces, in the mysteries of wedding science to public purposes, and in the character of civil-military relations as well. In this context, organizational and procedural designs are unusually important, it will be argued, since they determine the structure within which massive managerial and political control problems intersect. Moreover, there can be conflict between organizational strategy designed to produce efficient political decision processes and managerial strategy designed to achieve coherent control of weapon system development. Yet the organization for control of military R&D inevitably is a mixture of both purposes. It is argued here that the failure to cope explicitly and well with this paradox is the central public-policy problem of military R&D.

THE CHARACTER OF THE MILITARY RESEARCH
AND DEVELOPMENT PROCESS

Military R&D encompasses two quite different but overlapping
activities: investment in basic research and the "technology
base," and acquisition of new systems to support military
missions. Of the $13.5 billion proposed for military R&D in
1980, $436 million is intended for basic research and $2.3
billion for strengthening the technology base; the remaining
$10 billion is imbedded in the "front end" of the weapon
system acquisition process.(2)

That process involves much larger sums of money. In
fiscal 1980 the Carter administration seeks military procurement funds totaling $35.4 billion, and operation and main-
tenance funds totaling $40.2 billion, substantial portions of
which flow from weapon system acquisition decisions made
years ago within the context of military R&D.(3) Major systems such as the Trident or the MX may involve less than $1
billion in the R&D stages of development but $30-40 billion in
life cycle costs. A report by the General Accounting Office
in 1972 identified 141 major DOD systems in various stages of
acquisition which, when finally acquired, will have cost $163
billion simply to develop and purchase (and presumably much
more to own and operate).(4) Thus, from a management
point of view, careful design and control of the military R&D
process is one of the critical keys to successful financial and
programmatic management of the much more expensive systems
and military force structures which flow from that process.
The elaborate R&D decisional structure and process in the
Pentagon is a response to this enormous managerial challenge.

But the issue is more complex than this. The MX and
Trident are not simply expensive programs deserving of careful management. They are also: major commitments to specific
solutions of the complex problem of strategic nuclear deterrence; affirmation of roles and missions within and among the
military services; explicit choices about the importance of
strategic weapons relative to other military activities; explicit
choices about the importance of strategic weapons relative to
other public initiatives such as urban housing, national health
insurance, energy security or middle class tax relief; and, by
no means least, commitments to particular commercial enterprises which, as a result, will employ people in specific
places. In short, these weapon systems and the R&D process
which yields them lie in the center of the competition among
values, purposes, and programs inherent in the process of
public choice - by nature a political process. Organizational
and procedural imperatives designed to support this political
process are likely to be vastly different from, and perhaps in
conflict with, those designed to yield efficient management.

This conflict in organizational purposes is difficult to identify and extract from the extraordinary complexity of the acquisition process.   Armed Services Procurement Regulations (ASPR), the procedural bible governing R&D and procurement relationships between Pentagon agencies (including many government-owned laboratories) and defense industries, has grown from 100 to 3,000 pages.   Defense Department requests to industry for proposals for system development contracts sometimes contain 1,000 to 2,000 pages.   Contractor proposals in response are even more voluminous: one AWACS proposal for the Air Force contained 26,000 pages and involved 1,600 people in its preparation.   A proposal for the Navy's Harpoon missile system contained 35,000 pages.   Printed material for engine and airframe development for the C5A totaled 240,000 pages.(5)   The chairman of the R&D Subcommittee of the Senate Armed Services Committee once noted that the sub-committee - four senators and one staff person - in 1971 had to examine $8 billion in R&D funding proposals governing 4,000 projects grouped in 369 program elements.(6)

The managerial task of wedding uncertain technologies to vague and fluid missions is massive and demands sophis-ticated - and stable - management systems of extraordinary scale and complexity.   But in addition, the stakes involved - programmatic, institutional, financial, and frequently the highest national interests - guarantee that management of military R&D will be buffeted by intense political forces. These forces demand pluralistic organizational and procedural designs that conflict with managerial coherence: widespread participation, incremental decisions, and constant reexamina-tion of purpose, cost, and importance.

These conflicts in organizational purpose are endemic to the defense establishment as a whole.   Samuel P. Huntington established this point with great clarity in his seminal book, The Common Defense, nearly twenty years ago:

> The most distinctive, the most fascinating, and the most troublesome aspect of military policy is its Janus-like quality.   Indeed, military policy not only faces in two directions, it exists in two worlds. One is international politics, the world of the bal-ance of power, wars and alliances, the subtle and the brutal uses of force and diplomacy to influence the behavior of other states.   The principal cur-rency of this world is actual or potential military strength: battalions, weapons, and warships.   The other world is domestic politics, the world of in-terest groups, political parties, social classes, with their conflicting interests and goals.   The currency here is the resources of society: men, money, ma-terial.   Any major decision in military policy influ-

ences and is influenced by both worlds. A decision
made in terms of one currency is always payable in
the other.(7)

But the central importance of military R&D in the weapon
system acquisition process (and thus in military policy overall) in conjunction with the complexity of the technologies involved, present uniquely high-temperature problems for public policy and management.

RECENT HISTORY: PERSISTENT AND VEXING PROBLEMS

Since World War II the central problem in military R&D seems
to have been managing the elusive linkage between increasingly sophisticated and expensive technology on the one
hand, and military doctrine, force structure, and strategic
purpose on the other. In managerial theory the process is
linear and sequential: a military need is established; the
possibilities for technological achievement of that need are
identified, developed, and validated; prototype systems are
built, tested, and evaluated; cost and effectiveness data are
analyzed, a production decision made, and the system procured. Suitable decision controls are installed at key points
along the way.
     In practice, of course, the process is much messier than
this. Military needs are difficult to establish and change
over time; the process of translating a requirement into
technical possibilities is capricious and difficult to predict and
schedule; engineering development is fraught with uncertainties; setbacks occur in the form of performance shortfalls,
delays, and cost overruns; full-scale development and operational testing bring out mistakes in earlier stages of the
process. The result is that the sequential discipline required
for good management breaks down. The normal response to
management problems are management solutions. But the root
of the managerial problem is a deeper problem of political
process, and solutions are much harder to identify. What will
follow is likely to be a succession of "new" management strategies. To paraphrase Huntington's colorful analysis, military
R&D management may be subject to a foreign-exchange problem: its management currency may be redeemable only in the
currency of politics.
     The Pentagon's response to the difficulties of R&D man-
agement has mainly been a sequence of experiments in explicit
management strategy and implicit political strategy. The
modern history of these experiments may be said really to
begin in the early 1960s. Prior to Secretary Robert McNamara's appointment in 1961, the secretary of defense lacked

the power to intervene effectively in the weapon-system-acquisition policies of the services, except in cases where competition for roles and missions among services yielded service weapon systems vying for the same mission. Military R&D as an overall Department of Defense management concern in the context described here was a highly visible - but mainly hypothetical - issue.

McNamara's tenure at the Pentagon brought the Office of the Secretary of Defense (OSD) into the weapon-system-acquisition process in a serious way for the first time, largely through the installation of the planning, programming, budgeting system (PPBS) and McNamara's forceful use of it.

The major effect of McNamara's innovations was a fundamental shift in political design of organization and process. For the first time, OSD became an effective player in the weapon system acquisition process, positioned to challenge service dominance of that process. All of this is well documented elsewhere.(8) The new process focused attention on the requirements process and sought to bring to bear on decisions sophisticated analytical techniques and cost-effectiveness concerns. There were substantial managerial improvements in the sense that validation of requirements (which tend to trigger and shape acquisition programs) was subjected to systematic review and analysis, and the generation of alternative means of meeting requirements came to be an accepted managerial practice.

But in retrospect these gains may have been illusory and overwhelmed by the political effects of OSD's vigorous participation in the R&D process. The F-111 fighter-bomber and C-5A cargo aircraft provide striking - but different - examples.

In keeping with his efforts to develop stronger conventional warfare capabilities, McNamara in early 1961 directed the Navy and the Air Force to merge their plans for new tactical fighters. The Navy wanted an aircraft for fleet air defense. The Air Force wanted a high-speed fighter-bomber capable of nuclear interdiction. McNamara wanted an agile fighter capable of supporting conventional air and ground operations.(9) McNamara succeeded in establishing a joint Air Force-Navy program, but he failed to get the airplane he sought. The plane ultimately produced retained the Air Force nuclear interdiction capability, was too big and heavy for Navy carrier use, could carry relatively few convention munitions, and was too slow and cumbersome for air-to-air combat. The Navy procured no F-111s after spending $375 million for development, and went on to procure the F-14. The Air Force bought one-third the number of aircraft planned and went on to build the F-15.(10)

From a management point of view, the F-111 program was a disaster - performance objectives were never achieved, and the unit cost of the airplane was double what had been planned. But the causes of this failure were political, not managerial. Neither service really accepted a compromise. The Navy's physical and performance requirements were simply added to those of the Air Force, with the result that it became impossible to build the planned airplane. Neither the Navy nor the Air Force was prepared to abandon its conception of the impact of roles and missions on fighter design. McNamara had enough political influence to give the director of defense research and engineering (DDR&E) bureaucratic credibility as advocate of a joint fighter program. But he lacked the political resources to define his own alternatives or to force the services to cooperate in making the program produce what he wanted. Management systems could not cope with the effects on F-111 development of this political failure.

The C-5A program yielded similar effects. The Office of Systems Analysis in OSD noted that airlift and sea-lift capabilities typically received low priority among the services because these capabilities involved services provided by the Air Force and Navy to the Army. Based on a series of studies in 1963 and 1964, Systems Analysis proposed a larger mix of airlift and sea-lift capabilities for rapid reinforcement of allies and U.S. forces overseas.(11) From this general posture, Systems Analysis came to support the concept of the C-5A - largely a creature of its own design. Here again McNamara possessed sufficient political resources to reach for and control the decision to develop and procure the aircraft, but not enough to control the implementation of his decision. Systems Analysis was mandated and staffed to assess cost-effectiveness but not to manage the design and development of aircraft. The Air Force, which possessed both the mandate and staff capabilities, withheld its vigorous support for the program.

The result might have been another F-111 with lowest-common-denominator capabilities but for the intervention of a new weapon-system-acquisition process known as total package procurement concept (TPPC). Under TPPC a contractor undertook for a fixed price to perform all development and produce the initial batch of systems. The Defense Department expected the new process to curb the cost growth of the 1950s and shorten acquisition time as well.(12) Applied to the C-5A, the new concept gave OSD an independent agency (the contractor) to manage the development of the aircraft without the active support of the Air Force. The result was that the aircraft was built generally to Systems Analysis mission specifications, but with serious structural deficiencies and major cost overruns. The lack of design and program management competence in Systems Analysis (and the lack of a license to acquire that competence) created a gap in the development process, which, with the accelerated development procedures of TPPC, brought unfortunate consequences. A new management concept designed for one purpose proved disastrous in the face of the political context within which it was implemented.

What do these examples indicate? First McNamara's organizational innovations permanently changed the political process within which weapon systems are acquired, by establishing OSD as a strong force in Defense Department resource management decisions. But the services retained substantial political resources of their own, particularly with regard to implementation of McNamara's decisions. What McNamara sought in the currency of managerial innovation in decision making, he failed to achieve because he lacked real legal tender - the political currency for implementation.

Second, the failure of the McNamara innovations to curb cost growth and performance shortfalls - a political problem - triggered a wave of managerial experiments, all of which dealt only implicitly if at all with the political setting and which thus have largely been failures. The succession of such experiments continues to this day.

Third, the failure of McNamara's acquisition-management innovations brought Congress to intervene much more actively in the weapon system acquisition process. This has had the effect, among others, of making Congress a vigorous participant in the R&D process, greatly complicating both R&D politics and management.

Fourth, the political effects of McNamara's centralization of authority in the Pentagon and of the management flaws in the weapon system acquisition process prompted the Nixon administration to adopt new political and managerial strategies. OSD lost much of its political influence over the strategy-force-structure nexus to the National Security Council and its influence over the force-structure-weapon-systems connection back to the services. The Office of Systems Analysis was downgraded, reflecting reduced emphasis on PPBS as a means of political and managerial control over service programs. Instead, OSD, under the leadership of Deputy Secretary David Packard, concentrated its efforts on direct management of the weapon-system-acquisition process.

Packard returned day-to-day program management to the services, but sought OSD essential management control through the definition of "milestones" - key decision points in the weapon system acquisition process which would permit program review by OSD. Packard established the Defense System Acquisition Review Council (DSARC) consisting of key OSD officials responsible for different functional aspects of the acquisition process, who would direct a coherent acquisition management process.

Packard also installed more conservative acquisition management strategies ("fly before you buy") and better contracting procedures to eliminate the acquisition compression which bedevilled the C-5A and the Navy F-14. In effect Packard abandoned the resource allocation decision mechanism of McNamara's PPBS and erected alongside it a new organizational structure based on focused program management. Ironically, the managerial improvements he sought largely escaped his grasp - again for reasons of faulty political design of organizational arrangements. While the new DSARC process gave the appearance of stronger OSD managerial control combined with service initiative and expertise, its political leverage was relatively weaker than that of the PPBS system; installed alongside PPBS, it yielded overall a weaker structure still.

A key flaw in the Packard DSARC process lay in its initial intervention in weapon-system acquisition. DSARC Milestone 1 (DSARC I), as it was called, involved validating a system concept through paper studies or hardware development.(13) Intervention at this stage assumed that a mission requirement had been established in terms of a specific weapon-system concept, and what was to be validated at DSARC I was whether or not technologies existed to support that concept. The flaw was that the services possessed the political resources to eviscerate the managerial purposes of DSARC I, using it to legitimize very specific hardware specifications and gaining substantial leverage in the PPBS process.

The services had long before devised methods of hiding the early stages of weapon system development until design was complete and political support assembled. One such ploy had been the practice of breaking down a planned new weapon system into components, each of which could be developed independently under program descriptions whose titles were quite technical and did not indicate plans for a major weapon system. For example, the Commission on Government Procurement in 1972 described the Army's use of this practice in the mid-1960s as it sought to fund the development of an armed helicopter before the program had been approved.

Although the AH-56 Cheyenne helicopter appeared for large-scale funding in 1965, it began years earlier in exploratory development under a project titled "aircraft suppressive fire." Another project called "air mobility" also helped finance this early armed helicopter exploration. In about 1963, the project was moved into an advanced development project listed as "aircraft suppressive fire" and in 1964 became an engineering development activity identified as the "aircraft suppressive fire system."

This was changed later to "weapons helicopter" and
still later to the "advanced aerial fire support system." With each change, the identifying project
number was changed.(14)

Under the DSARC process the practice evidently grew as the
services became aware that the key to successful program
advocacy lay in defining in as much detail as possible how a
general mission need or requirement should be met with a
specific weapon system. Thus one statement of a mission
need not only called for a manned aircraft but also specified
the following characteristics:

* Takeoff and landing distances
* Combat radius and combat profile with weapon loads and
  energy gains for manuevering
* Sea-level speed
* Maximum speed
* Ferry range
* Eight separate design point performance specifications
* Thrust-to-weight ratio
* Structural load factors
* Fire control systems for specified missile types, gun,
  and other functions
* Navigational system accuracy limits and number of pres-
  ent checkpoints
* Guns better than those in operation
* External fuel tank capacity
* Month of latest IOC
* Other system performance characteristics(15)

In addition, DSARC I examined each candidate system
without regard to competing uses for scarce DOD funds - that
process lay within the province of the director of program
analysis and evaluation, who managed PPBS. While the director sat in DSARC meetings, he lacked procedural and
political control over decisions. The result was a bow-wave
effect in which the number of systems in development far exceeds what the PPBS system could conceivably bless for full
funding.(16)
Packard himself evidently felt the effects of the DSARC
political design flaws as he wrestled with the Navy over the
Trident program. Originally labeled ULMS, the project was
conceived as a missile program to extend the range of under-
water ballistic missiles and therby reduce the vulnerability of
Polaris and Poseidon submarines. The project was assigned
in the late 1960s to the Special Project Office (SPO), the
Navy agency reknowned for its successful development of the
Polaris.(17) There the missile program quickly evolved into a
new submarine and missile program. A struggle between SPO

and Admiral Hyman G. Rickover, who controlled naval nuclear power-plant programs, ensued over control of the new Trident program. SPO wanted a submarine using an off-the-shelf power reactor, which would have effectively kept Rickover out of the program. Rickover wanted a new, much more powerful reactor to drive a huge new submarine - and by engaging the support of the submarine commanders, he won.(18) Efforts by the undersecretary of the Navy and the chief of naval operations to develop a less expensive, equally effective option failed.

At this point Packard sought to intervene by adopting the cheaper option in his September 1971 development concept paper - the document which establishes the mission requirement before development begins. At first Packard's finesse worked, but it was eventually overwhelmed by White House intervention through the PPBS system. President Nixon had announced the Moscow SALT summit, and in October 1971 asked Defense Secretary Melvin Laird to increase substantially strategic-forces spending, in order to allay conservative fears about the emerging SALT treaty. The Navy would accept acceleration only of the original Trident program - not Packard's option - and his finesse was overturned in the budget process.(19)

What were the effects of Packard's reforms? There were several, on two levels. First, Packard's design and operation of the DSARC process created a more sustained OSD preoccupation with R&D and acquisition management. Conservative acquisition strategies involving less concurrency, more prototyping, and more extensive test and evaluation became the rule. Better cost-estimation techniques and concerns about life-cycle costs and affordability emerged as management issues within OSD. The DSARC became the dominant organizational forum for system-acquisition management.

But in organizational-politics terms, the Packard reforms - in conjunction with other events and developments of the time - produced a net decline in OSD's capacity to influence the weapon system acquisition process. First, decentralization of program initiative back to the services meant that the services would again define system requirements, and by the time concepts reached the DSARC process, options would be squeezed out in an effort to lock in the results of intraservice bargaining.

Second, the centralization of authority in the White House, when the president, OMB, or the NSC chose to exercise it, and the increasing vigor of congressional intervention sapped the DSARC process of the political coherence necessary to put flesh on the mangement reforms. Moreover, the existence of a DSARC program-management process alongside, but partly independent of, the PPBS resource-allocation process guaranteed that the overall organizational design

within OSD would become pluralistic and redundant - in effect
a willy-nilly response to the political forces set loose by
McNamara in 1961. Over time it became impossible to follow
the progression of decision commitment envisioned in the
DSARC sequence. Those who lost in decisions taken in
DSARC I and II would be back in DSARC III for another try
at the same issues. It was difficult to prevent this because
the availability of PPBS channels made it possible to sidestep
DSARC decisions.

The Packard innovations also produced a more subtle,
and ultimately perhaps more significant, result. McNamara in
1961 created an organizational and process design which,
though labeled "managerial" and "analytical," was in fact
profoundly political (in the sense used in this analysis).
Packard's reforms constituted a uniquely managerial design,
relatively insensitive to the flow of political action which sur-
rounded it. His legacy has been a persistent and increasing
tendency within OSD to seek managerial solutions to what are
really political problems of organizational design. A key
question is whether this legacy continues under Defense Secretary Harold Brown and the Carter administration.

The background for Secretary Brown's changes was set
in the context of the reports of the Blue Ribbon Defense
Panel(20) and the Commission on Government Procurement.(21) Both argued for substantial reorganization of the
weapon system acquisition process to seek more effective management of the process. The most important development
resulting from the procurement commission in particular has
been the creation of the Office of Federal Procurement Policy
(OFPP) in OMB and the promulgation of OMB Circular A109.
Among other things A109 requires designation of an "acquisition executive" within each agency and establishes a mission-
element need statement (MENS) from the agency head docu-
menting the relationship between a proposed major system
concept and the agency's mission.(22) Although A109 is cast
in managerial terms, it is based on a frank assessment by the
procurement commission of the political structure within which
R&D and acquisition decisions are taken. OFPP Administrator
Lester A. Fettig made this point clear in recent congressional
testimony:

> To characterize the commission's findings,
> there were two underlying problems. First, im-
> provements were needed in the management struc-
> ture across the federal government to determine
> decision authority during the course of a system
> acquisition program. What was found was confusion
> in decision responsibilities. To oversimplify some-
> what, the Commission found Congress often playing
> a detailed design management role while the agen-

cies sometimes seemed to preempt policy-making and
Defense strategy decisions.

A second basic conclusion was that all the
common defects in our weapons programs - cost
overruns, schedule slippages, performance deficiencies, buy-ins, bail outs, and contractual contests -
were all symptomatic of the problems sewn into the
program earlier at the front end.

The Commission found a very poor job being
done across the board in defining program needs
and goals. Both Congress and the agency head
were found to be playing a relatively unstructured,
undisciplined role with the action mainly focused
around the military departments and industry,
where for many years and with millions of dollars,
weapons requirements evolved. This process extended into the basic exploration of alternatives,
quickly foreclosing options without any regular in-
volvements by the agency head or the Congress
demand [sic] and preserve a range of options.(23)

Secretary Brown has attempted to improve upon the management reforms initiated by Packard in the directions suggested by A109 and the Blue Ribbon Defense Panel. The
director of defense research and engineering (DDR&E) has
now become the undersecretary for research and engineering
(USD/R&E) and, as the Defense Department acquisition executive, now manages for OSD the weapon system acquisition
process. A milestone "0" has been installed at the front end
of the DSARC process ("DSARC 0") to ensure that for major
systems there exists a formal process leading to Secretary
Brown's signature on a mission-element need statement for the
proposed weapon system.

As management improvements, the new organizational arrangements look impressive. A single executive has been
made responsible for the entire sequence of acquisition
events. Much more attention is given to systematic examination of the mission need for new systems before DSARC I.
However, the fundamental political problems inherent in the
organizational design of OSD, and service control of systems
acquisition, remain.

One of the implicit political purposes of the original
DSARC had been systematic OSD control of the process by
which a weapon system passed from the R&D advocates of a
program to the users who would have to live with its procurement. It had been assumed that over a period of time
the DDR&E, as manager of the R&D process, would become an
advocate of systems successfully developed and might not
objectively reflect the concerns of users in approaching
procurement decisions. To guard against this, the DDR&E

chaired the DSARC I and II meetings, but the DSARC III
(production decision) meeting was chaired by the assistant
secretary of defense for installation and logistics (ASD/I&L),
who represented the users.   In practice the process rarely
worked as planned, for several reasons:

•   User support for a system was negotiated within the
     responsible service beforehand, so that the ASD/I&L had
     little leverage to oppose poor systems.
•   DDR&E controlled OSD resources for both development
     test and evaluation (DT&E) and operational test and
     evaluation (OT&E), so that test results important to the
     user were conducted in effect by the developer.
•   No one possessed the analytical resources or the
     information necessary to question DDR&E's technical
     judgment.

     Secretary Brown's reorganization combined installation
and logistics with manpower and reserve affairs under the
assistant secretary, presumably to integrate resource management.   But, in conjunction with designation of the undersecretary for research and engineering as DOD acquisition
executive, this arrangement creates a new organizational bar-
rier within OSD between development and acquisition on the
one hand and the user on the other.   Secretary Brown initially sought to compensate for this by transferring operational test and evaluation from the undersecretary for research and engineering to the assistant secretary for program
analysis and evaluation in 1977.   An expanded test-and-
evaluation function under the control of the analytic manager,
who had no stakes in either the development or the procurement of a weapon system, would help keep the DSARC process honest.
     Unfortunately, the arguments for a coherently managed
acquisition process began to upset the political balance within
OSD.   After months of negotiations and maneuvering between
the Office of Research and Engineering and that of Program
Analysis and Evaluation for transfer of the staff resources for
operational test and evalution, the plan was abandoned in late
1978, and operational test and evaluation was returned to the
undersecretary for research and engineering on the grounds
of acquisition-management efficiency.(24)   Apparently some of
the impetus for this decision came from the report of a
Defense Science Board Acquisition Cycle Task Force (the 1977
Summer Study).   The task force was charged with determining whether the acquisition cycle was growing longer, and
if so, what the underlying causes were.(25)   The task force
suggested a shortening of the front end of the acquisition
cycle through "flexible" application of A109, increased concurrency, and reduced application of operational test and

evaluation (OT&E) as a mechanism for arbitration between developer and user. The task force's comments are illuminating.

> The inventors of OT&E are saying, in effect, "The development process some way or other comes up with products that the user doesn't like. We can save a lot of money if we can find out which they are and then not put them into production." This approach is clearly wrong, since the objective of the entire business is to get needed capabilities into the hands of the fighting forces in a timely manner, in order to give them the tools to respond to the threat at any given time. The present OT&E philosophy seems to encourage deciding at this late point in the acquisition cycle that we are better off with nothing than with the wrong thing. To accept the waste of what may have been a very large expenditure of development money if only production money can be saved appears to the Task Force to be a dismal approach to defense systems acquisition, at best.
> OT&E supporters are swimming upstream. The idea behind the whole thing should not be to put a stop to the acquisition process, but to assist in getting needed equipment into the field.(26)

Secretary Brown has not yet acted on the Task force report (other than to restore operational test and evaluation to the undersecretary for research and engineering). However it would appear that events to date point toward an OSD organizational emphasis on managerial efficiency and away from political effectiveness. Here again the Acquisition Cycle Task Force report is instructive.

> It was determined on the basis of a number of weapon system acquisition program case studies that it doesn't actually take any longer to <u>do</u> something; it just takes longer to obtain the necessary approvals and acquire funding to do it and to get to the deployment stage once the development is finished. These decision delays do not take the form simply of more time for the decision maker to decide; they are manifested by additional complication in the decision process - more levels of review and approval, additional steps in the system definition and development process and therefore more decision points, demands for more analyses, more studies, more justification, more tests, and more evaluation of results.

In general, the length of time it takes to do
something is dependent both on how hard it is to
do it and on how badly society wants to have it
done. It is not apparently inherently more difficult
to do things than it used to be. Although the
things we do today are often larger and more complex, we bring better tools and better knowledge to
the task. The trouble lies rather in the growing
lack of desire of the society to do certain kinds of
things, such as to build modern weapon systems or
to construct nuclear power plants. There are always certain people who strongly advocate doing
almost anything - and others who are as adamantly
opposed to doing it.

The change in society's desires in recent years
is in part due to the change in the relative numbers of such people, but probably is more importantly a result of the general attitude of the vast
majority of the people who are not actively engaged
in the struggle but whose sympathies determine the
rules under which the struggle takes place. In
recent years, society's sympathies have moved away
from the doers toward the opposers, thereby increasing their social and legal standing, and their
ability to slow down or, in come cases, to stop the
activities of the doers altogether. From the point
of view of the doers, it is harder and harder to get
things done these days - they still want them done
as badly as ever. But from the point of view of
society, however, it is the desire which has
changed, not the difficulty of doing things.(27)

In fact the task force has a point: part of the organizational
design problem in recent years is a political structure which
has created severe managerial problems. The endless sequence of reviews, interventions, and delays caused by the
struggle for access to decisions both within and outside the
Pentagon is a program manager's nightmare. More and more
often, program managers must spend their time on political
advocacy and less on actual program management. The result
is less adept management of increasingly complex technology,
and thus more cost overruns and performance shortfalls; increasing efforts to lock in detailed weapon system designs
early in the acquisition cycle to secure service programs, and
thus a decline in technological competition; and, in response,
more and more reviews and interventions to counter the effects of political advocacy.

But the task force is wrong to think that the kinds of
managerial streamlining involved in compressing the front end
of the acquisition cycle will solve this problem. More exten-

sive use of concurrency may save funds in the development
process, but it is likely to mean expensive redevelopment in
the procurement phase. It also means fewer opportunities for
OSD control of the process. Less independent OT&E reduces
delays and eliminates costs of redundant testing, but it also
removes from OSD an opportunity to ensure that the weapon
system performs as expected (or that the testing process is
honest). In short, compression of the front end of the acquisition cycle would be a program developer's dream; to all
the other participants in the process - OSD, OMB, and the
Congress - it would be a nightmarish return to all the evils
which brought McNamara to inject OSD forcefully into the
process in the first place.

If the logic of all of this holds true, then the apparent
propensity of the Carter administration to resolve these problems through managerial redesign of organization and process
is unlikely to succeed. What then might be done? That
question is dealt with in the concluding section, where the
answer proposed is that good organizational design alone will
not exorcise all the demons in the weapon system acquisition
process, but the lack of it is almost sure to keep them there.

THOUGHTS ON ORGANIZATIONAL DESIGN

The central political feature of the weapon system acquisition
process is that its control inevitably resides mainly in the
hands of the services. No one else in the system has the
information and the financial and staff resources to wield the
day-to-day influence over programs that "micromanagement"
permits. Moreover, no one can match the unique claim to
control of the military-requirements process that the wearing
of a uniform conveys. Thus the struggle for civilian influence over the acquisition process will always be uphill. And,
given the differences in values and purposes among the
various political constituencies which surround the Pentagon,
civilian involvement will inevitably be diffuse, fragmented,
and pluralistic. How then can sufficient order be brought
into political design so that good management practices may
flourish?

The answer seems mainly to lie in the organizational
design of OSD. The secretary of defense potentially has
more influence with and more coherent control over the services than have OMB, the NSC, or Congress. The Secretary
of Defense can have more influence with the president and
Congress than the services have, if he develops the political
resources to exercise it. McNamara knew this very well, and
Secretary Brown evidently does too. But the conflict between
managerial coherence and political order - when not addressed

in OSD organizational design - tends to reduce rather than expand the secretary's influence.

Five principles might be usefully established to govern organizational design (for the purpose discussed here) in OSD:

- Key staff agencies in OSD should be organized to reflect (1) the advocacy interests of the services; (2) Defense Department-wide interests in policy and management coordination; and (3) the secretary's interests in forcing key decisions up to him and keeping processes honest.
- Decision processes should be designed to display conflicting interests accurately and efficiently before the secretary so that he can correctly gauge the real stakes involved and make decisions that are enforceable.
- The weapon system acquisition decision process and the resource allocation process should be linked in ways that strengthen the quality and enforceability of the secretary's decisions in each process.
- Where possible, incentives for effective performance on the part of the services should be substituted for direct OSD management control of service activities.
- The character of the acquisition process should be such that it efficiently distinguishes for the secretary between systems which can be safely (and effectively) developed via a short cycle, high-concurrency strategy versus those which will require a carefully staged, conservative strategy with extensive mid-cycle test and evaluation, prototyping, and low initial rates of production.

The application of these principles (or any others) should be heavily conditioned by the preferences and personal style of the secretary. But given that, one can hypothesize some elements of an organizational design embodying the principles.

First, with regard to the DSARC process, the decisions to validate a system requirement and acquisition strategy, to proceed to full-scale development, and to begin procurement (in effect the responsibilities of the acquisition executive stipulated by A109) should not be made below the deputy secretary of defense. Conferring the acquisition-executive authority on any of the undersecretaries or assistant secretaries with functional responsibilities (and staff resources) will inevitably threaten the integrity of the process and make it less accessible to the secretary.

Second, the secretary needs competent staff support of his stakes in the DSARC process. This means strong technical and analytical staff in the offices of both the undersecretary and the assistant secretary, who should be equipped to question each other's judgments. Similarly, it is important to

elevate the status of the director of operational test and
evaluation to assistant-secretary level, to strengthen that
function as a mechanism for safeguarding the secretary's
interests in keeping the sequence of acquisition decisions
honest.

Third, control of each of the DSARC milestone decisions
should rest with the OSD staff agency most responsible for
the consequences of the decisions taken.   Thus DSARC 0
should be chaired by the undersecretary for policy and
staffed by the assistant secretary for program analysis and
evaluation.   DSARC I and II should be chaired and staffed by
the undersecretary for research and engineering.   DSARC III
should be chaired by the deputy secretary; IIIA, the decision
point for low-level production, should be staffed by the assistant secretary for operational test and evaluation; and IIIB,
the decision point for full-rate production, should be staffed
by the assistant secretary for manpower, reserve affairs, and
logistics.

Fourth, with regard to linkage between the systems acquisition process and the resource allocation process, three
kinds of links may be useful.   First, as soon as a weapon
system enters the DSARC process (that is, a "go" decision in
DSARC 0) it should be registered in the PPBS process as a
claimant against the "planning wedge" of uncommitted resources potentially available to the defense budget in subsequent years.   How such a planning wedge would relate to the
FYDP is of course a matter of critical importance to the PPBS
process, and is another issue.   But the point to be made
here is that the first decision made in the DSARC process
should be registered immediately in the PPBS process.

A second link has to do with coordination of DSARC
decisions (especially II and III) with programming and budget
decisions in the PPBS process.   The widely accepted notion
that DSARC provides the "authorization" for weapons system
acquisitions and that the PPBS provides the "appropriation" is
a weak concept because it separates programmatic decisions
from budgetary ones and thereby vitiates the strength of the
PPBS as a resource-allocation mechanism to weight programs
and budgets together.   Moreover, separating DSARC and
PPBS decisions brings political pluralism to bear in precisely
the wrong way: battles lost in either DSARC or PPBS can be
fought again in the other forum, and a powerful set of forces
for multiple reviews, overturned decisions, and excessive
participation is set in motion.

A better linkage would be to coordinate some - but not
all - DSARC II and III decisions with the schedule of the
PPBS programming and budget cycle.   Thus the secretary
would schedule decisions for major systems so that a decision
is registered in both processes at once.   It might be possible, for example, to compress the PPBS program and budget

reviews into a single major-issue review period, in which
DSARC II and III decision meetings were also scheduled.
How this might be done is a matter of detailed architecture of
the PPBS; but if applied successfully, the principle would
reduce unnecessary redundancy in DOD decision making and
strengthen the enforcement of both DSARC and PPBS decisions.

The third link would be procedural, to strengthen further both DSARC and the PPBS. In order to be considered
in the PPBS, the secretary may require that system acquisitions be in compliance with the process requirements of A109.
In fact this notion has been tested at the insistence of OMB
during the fiscal year 1980 budget review, but its effects are
not yet clear. It also may be possible to establish a reverse
linkage in which acquisitions facing DSARC decisions could
not be considered unless certain procedural requirements had
been met within PPBS.

The detailed design of these linkages would have to be
carefully worked out, but the intent would be to use the two
processes to reinforce one another rather than weaken the
secretary's authority by allowing one to vitiate the other.

Fifth, all of these organizational tune-ups would have to
be matched by changes in the substance of acquisition-management theory. Development of technologically complex major
systems will inevitably be difficult, fraught with uncertainties, and more time consuming and expensive than expected.
The perceived nature of the threat, military doctrine and
tactics, and resources available for acquisition are sure to
change during the development period, requiring constant
reevaluation of the merits and progress of the system. That
is how it should be, and efforts to isolate the acquisition
management process from such pressures in the name of coherent and sound management are sure to introduce crippling
distortions into the political structure of the process.

Moreover, it is foolish to impose tight managerial and
fiscal constraints on what is unavoidably a messy and uncertain process. Lack of funds to permit flexible acquisition-
management decisions as more information is gathered about
the behavior of new technology is sure to mean makeshift,
ill-considered decisions early in development, and greatly increased prospects for costly fixes in the future.

And finally, the benefits of competition as a means of
reducing costs and achieving better technological ingenuity
seem, as a matter of historical evidence, to be so great as to
warrant vigorous insistence on its use in as many stages of
the acquisition process as possible. No management system
can eliminate the unexpected surprises which inhere in the
application of technology. But competition greatly reduces
the effect of those surprises. And competition reduces the
tendency of the political environment to produce capricious

disruptions of acquisition management as well, since decisions can be made on a more solid base of fact and evidence.

As a final point it should be noted that organizational design is no more than a framework within which people and the agencies relate to one another. Organization (and reorganization) is not a substitute for political leadership and managerial skill. But faulty organizational design can make it impossible for people to do their jobs effectively. Good organizational design, on the other hand, can be constructive rather than destructive; can provide a political context within which good management practices can flourish; and can facilitate the circumstances in which what people do in their own self-interest yields a publicly laudable result.

NOTES

(1) Figures refer to budget authority, not outlays. See *The Budget of the United States Government, Fiscal Year 1980* (Washington, D.C.: U.S. Government Printing Office, 1979), pp. 24, 98.

(2) *Special Analyses, Budget of the United States Government, Fiscal Year 1980* (Washington, D.C.: U.S. Government Printing Office, 1979), p. 306. (Figures are in budget authority.)

(3) *The Budget*, p. 98 (figures in budget authority). Note that personnel costs, which also are affected by weapon system acquisition, are not included here.

(4) U.S. Comptroller General, *Acquisition of Major Weapons Systems*, July 1972, p. 65.

(5) *Report of the Commission on Government Procurement* 2 (Washington, D.C.: U.S. Government Printing Office, 1972), p. 137.

(6) Ibid., p. 130.

(7) Samuel P. Huntington, *The Common Defense* (New York: Columbia University Press, 1961), p. 1.

(8) See for example, Alain C. Enthoven and K. Wayne Smith, *How Much is Enough: Shaping the Defense Program 1961-1969* (New York: Harper and Row, 1971).

(9) *Commission on the Organization of the Government for the Conduct of Foreign Policy*, 4 (Washington, D.C.: U.S. Government Printing Office, 1975), pp. 119-125.

(10) Ibid., p. 118.

(11) Ibid., pp. 184-185.

(12) *Report on the Commission on Government Procurement* 2, p. 158.

(13) Ibid., p. 136.

(14) Ibid., p. 130.

(15) Ibid., pp. 98-99.

(16) Report on the Acquisition Cycle Task Force, Defense
      Science Board 1977 Summer Study, p. 83.
(17) Commission on the Organization of the Government for
      the Conduct of Foreign Policy 4, p. 176.
(18) Ibid., pp. 176-177.
(19) Ibid., pp. 178-180.
(20) Report to the President and the Secretary of Defense
      on the Department of Defense, July 1970.
(21) Report of the Commission on Government Procurement 2,
      p. 137.
(22) Office of Management and Budget Circular A109, April
      5, 1976.
(23) Statement before the Subcommittee on Research and De-
      velopment, House Committee on Armed Services, Novem-
      ber 2, 1977.
(24) This account of events is based on author discussions
      with officials in USD/R&E and ASD/PA&E.
(25) Report of the Acquisition Cycle Task Force, Defense
      Science Board 1977 Summer Study.
(26) Ibid., pp. 57-58.
(27) Ibid., pp. 35-36.

10 The Decision-Making Role of Congress*
Judith Reppy
Franklin A. Long

Congress, with its control over the RDT&E budget of DOD and its general responsibility for program oversight, stands at the center of the decision-making process for programs of military R&D. However carefully the Department of Defense prepares its programs and budget, it can only implement them after congressional authorization and appropriation of funds. The constitutional assignment to vote funds and authorize the size of the armed forces gives Congress the potential for great power to control the force structure and defense posture of the United States.

Congressional oversight of the programs of military R&D is not a simple task. The RDT&E budget is large and it is presented in considerable detail. The technical complexity of the programs can be daunting to a group whose members are for the most part graduates of law schools. To question the programs in the budget is to challenge the expertise and judgment of the senior military officers who submit the programs and testify in their support. For these reasons and because national security issues are fundamental to the existence of the nation, there is a tendency to go along with the DOD's budget requests, even when the sums of money are very large and competing pressures from nonmilitary needs very great.

---

*Many of the ideas of this chapter were presented to the workshop by Larry Smith who for several years was a staff member of the Subcommittee for R&D of the Senate Armed Services Committee. The authors gratefully acknowledge their debt to Mr. Smith and to the other participants who discussed his presentation.

But Congress cannot evade its responsibility. It is precisely because large sums of public money are at stake that congressional oversight is so important. The further peculiar significance of military R&D is that the R&D projects are the principal determinants of future weapons. The relations between military hardware, military strength, and national security are not rigid, but they are sufficiently strong that the decisions on the RDT&E budget can have significant impact on force structure for years to come.

The relationship between spending for military R&D and greater military strength is complex; more weapons developments do not automatically equate with more national security. The allocation of resources to new technology has to be balanced with the funds available for procurement of currently needed weapons, and must additionally allow for the implicit commitment to future procurement of the systems that stem from the R&D. Just as important, the military utility of new systems should be balanced against the effect they may have on international stability and future security in a world where other countries can and do react to U.S. technological initiatives.

Unfortunately, Congress does not analyze these larger issues in a regular or systematic fashion. Instead, particular problems - for example, the needs of NATO - may be taken up in great detail with special hearings and reports, only to be dropped in the next budget cycle. Relying, as they do, mainly on Pentagon witnesses, the armed services committees rarely hear a rounded analysis of the United States' international position, strengths, and weaknesses, and the members tend to lose sight of the broader context of national security. So long as this is true, and despite the huge effort expended during the presentation and discussion of the defense budget, the quality of congressional oversight will remain deficient.

But granting the existence of continuing problems and unmet challenges, there is no doubt that Congress now plays a larger and more effective role in analyzing military programs and setting budgets than it did in the past. Congress has moved beyond the earlier tradition that had it merely responding to executive initiatives in matters of foreign policy and national security. It is no longer constrained by lack of information or staff support from making its own analyses and proposing its own solutions; increasingly, it has done so.(1) With its new willingness to challenge the recommendations of the executive branch, Congress has become an important arena for decision making for military R&D.

RECENT TRENDS IN CONGRESSIONAL OVERSIGHT

Before 1959 only the military-construction appropriation in the Department of Defense's budget was subject to annual authorization, and in practice the only regular scrutiny of the R&D programs was done by the House Appropriations Committee. In general, the emphasis was on the budget-making aspect of the oversight function, with special congressional hearings held only when a problem achieved high visibility, as, for example, when the Senate Armed Services Committee held hearings on the status of the satellite and missile programs in November and December of 1957.

Throughout the 1960s, congress steadily expended its oversight of the Department of Defense's budget and programs, including those for military R&D. After 1963 the entire RDT&E appropriation had to be authorized, and annual hearings on the R&D budget were held by the armed services committees in both houses. In 1968 when Senator Stennis became chairman of the Senate Armed Services Committee, he established a subcommittee for military R&D, with Senator McIntyre as its first chairman. The House Armed Services Committee has also established a special subcommittee for military R&D. The latest additions to the oversight activities are the congressional budget committees which were created by the Congressional Budget Act of 1974. This act aimed to give Congress a synoptic view of the federal budget like that provided to the executive branch by the Office of Management and Budget. Budget committees in both the House and Senate now review the defense budget as part of their overall look at the federal budget prior to setting a congressional ceiling. Where once only the House Appropriations Committee looked in detail at the RDT&E budget, it is now reviewed by six different congressional committees, three each in the Senate and House. Every year scores of witnesses, most of them from DOD, testify before these committees, and the printed record of hearings for the RDT&E program runs to thousands of pages.

An essential element of the enlarged scope of congressional activities has been the growth of professional staffs and congressional support agencies. The staffs of the committees and of individual members have increased in number and in their level of professional training. The General Accounting Office and Congressional Research Service have been joined by the Congressional Budget Office and the Office of Technology Assessment as groups that do studies for Congress. As a consequence, the number of studies and analyses commissioned by members of Congress has grown.

The congressional committees concerned with the military budget differ in their style of action, depending on their

principal responsibilities and the personalities and interests of
the members and staff associated with them. In the armed
services committees of the House and Senate there has been a
shift away from purely budgetary concerns to programatic
aspects. The appropriations committees retain formal authority for appropriating funds, but their significance in program
analysis has diminish relatively as the armed services committees have become more active. In addition, overlapping
membership between committees reduced the likelihood of independent analysis by the appropriations committee.(2)

The important budget committees of Congress have
brought more members of both houses into contact with the
defense budget. But these committees have not taken up the
RDT&E budget in detail, being concerned, as they are, mainly with overall fiscal impacts. The armed services committees, and to a lesser extent the appropriations committees,
are still the places where most of the congressional oversight
of DOD programs occurs.

The congressional role in decision making for military
programs extends beyond formal hearings and authorization
and appropriation of funds. The coalition of proponents and
supporters that forms around each DOD program, whether it
be the question of a new aircraft carrier or some smaller issue such as selection of a contractor for an R&D project,
naturally turns for support to sympathetic groups within
Congress. Much of the so-called congressional micro-man-
agement is, in fact, stimulated by factions within the Pentagon trying to reverse, through selectively leaked information to Congress, unpalatable decisions made within the executive branch. In this sense many congressional actions on
weapons programs are an extension of internal decision
making by the Department of Defense.(3)

In the kaleidoscope of changing issues and shifting al-
liances, success depends on knowing who one's allies are and
in mastering the intricacies of congressional procedures. Experienced observers describe congressional decisions on military R&D programs as largely the product of an "inside game"
in which the important decisions are made in the relative ob-
scurity of the subcommittees. The subcommittee actions can
be thought of as levers that eventually move the entire Congress. Decisions made by the subcommittee are only rarely
reversed by the full committee, and it is even more rare for a
committee recommendation on military R&D to be overturned on
the floor. There is an "outside game," conducted through
the news media and by floor challenges to legislation, which,
although it gets a large amount of publicity, is in general
much less effective in shaping legislation than is the inside
game.

In this view of congressional procedure, the support of
a few key members of Congress may be all that is needed to

win legislative approval on an issue. The underlying reason is the overwhelming number of demands that impinge on each congressman and senator; the increases in availability of information and staff support that have made possible the enlarged role of Congress ultimately run up against the limits to the divisibility of the time and attention of individual members. The natural tendency of members is to go along with the decisions reached by the specialized subcommittees, which are presumed to have studied the matter more carefully than other members of congress can afford to do.

THE R&D SUBCOMMITTEES OF THE
ARMED SERVICES COMMITTEES

These two subcommittees have become the focal points for congressional oversight of the U.S. programs of military R&D. Both committees are large and active. Each has strong staff support. Their principal activity is consideration of the programs and budgets for research, development, test, and evaluation (RDT&E) by the Department of Defense, but they also analyze the military R&D programs of the Department of Energy and the military implications of the R&D efforts of the National Agency for Space and Aeronautics. In addition to lengthy annual budget hearings for RDT&E, each subcommittee holds occasional hearings on specific topics, and issues numerous staff reports.

The hearings of the subcommittees on the proposed RDT&E budgets are important in two ways. First, they force the armed services to develop persuasive arguments for their proposed programs, and one must assume that in the process a good many questionable projects are eliminated. Second, the subcommittees can give visibility to major problems and decisions within the program. The R&D subcommittee of the House Armed Services Committee has given particular attention to the problem of realistic program schedules and service commonality, as for example, in the Army-Navy guided projectile programs.(4) The analogous Senate subcommittee insisted on including in the DOD's budget for fiscal year 1972 funding for the development of the air-launched cruise missile, thus providing technological options that were called for later when the B-1 bomber was cancelled. The subcommittees have also frequently taken a hard position against developments which they have judged to be technically ill conceived; for example, the submarine-launched cruise missile.

Congress - in particular, members of the armed services committees and their subcommittees - can influence defense policy in ways more subtle than those captured by any analysis of formal votes. Not only do individual congressmen and senators and their staff members respond to the information that they receive from contacts within the Department of Defense and the defense industry, but the DOD reciprocally must be responsive to signals received from Congress. A kind of "law of anticipatory response" is at work at all levels of R&D decision making, since in most cases officials would prefer not to include in their budget requests projects that are likely to run into serious problems with congress. On one occasion in 1973, when the Senate subcommittee had been reversed by the full committee (in the case of the Trident II missile), Senator McIntyre went to the floor of the Senate with a proposal to moderate the pace of the missile development. His amendment was only narrowly defeated, and it led DOD to adopt a changed timetable for the missile in its program the following year.

The same principle operates within Congress and helps to explain the good record of the subcommittees in getting their decisions sustained by their parent committees and by full votes of the House and Senate. The success of positions adopted by the subcommittees in some measure reflects the political astuteness of their members in judging the temper of Congress. Here, the "outside game," which appears to have little direct influence on program decisions, can be important in influencing public opinion and hence the atmosphere in which programs are considered; the best example is the public debate on antiballistic missile programs in the early 1970s, a debate which clearly influenced congressional action. Most military R&D programs, however, do not attract much public attention, especially in their early stages; so, the recommendations of the subcommittees for military R&D normally have overriding influence.

In recent years the R&D subcommittee of the Senate Armed Services Committee has been developing a broader integrated approach to its analyses of R&D programs. This integrated effort has two aspects. The subcommittee has attempted to integrate vertically the logical elements of policy-making in a series of special hearings.(5) The hearings have typically begun with a statement of official policy, followed by the set of military requirements identified as needed to fulfill that policy, a baseline estimate of current capacilities, an intelligence estimate of the current threat, and, finally, a review of the relevant R&D programs in the budget. The other approach taken by the subcommittee might be termed horizontal integration. A single mission area is analyzed, with all R&D programs that relate to it included in the overview. These hearings study and compare the relevant programs of all three armed services, programs that otherwise would be considered in isolation, if at all.

These special subcommittee hearings have necessarily been developed as additions to the regular budget hearings.

Done properly, they require a great deal of time for preparation, both by the committee staff and by the Department of Defense witnesses. They serve the very important function, however, of highlighting the broad questions that the R&D programs raise, questions that are often ignored in the detailed examination of the individual items in the budget. The hearings can stimulate better program analysis and elimination of duplication by the Department of Defense, and serve as a vehicle for education within DOD as well as for Congress. Programs can be considered in an atmosphere free of the fixation on budget levels that is inevitable in the annual hearings on budget-authorization legislation. At a more mundane level, the special hearings have provided an occasion for bringing together persons from the different armed services who are working in the same mission area.

PROBLEM AREAS IN CONGRESSIONAL OVERSIGHT

Congressional oversight of DOD programs still falls short of the ideal of reviewing the whole RDT&E program in relation to military requirements and overall priorities for national security. The amount of attention paid to individual programs has grown enormously, but it is still fragmented; there is too little of the broader view that has been attempted by some of the hearings of the Senate Armed Services Committee.

The fragmentation of congressional attention is partly a result of political realities. Even as competing responsibilities make it difficult for a member of Congress to take the time to develop a comprehensive view of the RDT&E program, political concerns may impel him to give considerable attention to an individual project of concern to interests in his district. So long as DOD programs carry local effects on employment and income, individual members of Congress will take an interest in them.

There is, in addition, the legacy of the earlier focus of congressional oversight on budgetary accountability. This focus led to demands for more and more detailed budget data, so that now the RDT&E budget as presented to Congress lists more than 800 separate program elements and about 3,000 different projects. The result is an abundance of information, more than can be absorbed in most cases. Data on budgets and programs are also presented by mission area (a requirement of the 1974 Congressional Budget Act that was already a practice for the RDT&E budget), but not much use seems to be made of these data, perhaps because the coverage of the individual categories is constantly shifting.

Expanded staff and reference support services do not automatically lead to improved analyses. Too often, a study of a special problem may be commissioned and accepted with a principal view to the publicity value of the ensuing news release. Such studies dilute the efforts of the support organizations, and, inevitably, the quality of the studies produced is lowered. Congressional hearings require thousands of hours of preparation and witness time, yet the outcome is too often a set of apparently haphazard congressional questions and agency answers with little follow-up on the problems raised. The tendency of committees to duplicate hearings and witnesses adds to the wastefulness of these procedures.

More seriously, the frame of reference for congressional oversight of R&D programs is too narrow. The RDT&E budget ought to be considered as part of an overall investment strategy for defense needs, but the congressional focus on individual programs obscures this larger view. Segregating RDT&E into a separate budget appropriation has provided the R&D effort with high visibility, but, in a sense, has placed a fence around it, inhibiting analysis of the total weapons process. As a consequence, weapons have occasionally been developed which turn out to be too costly to buy. More commonly, many R&D programs are either delayed or the products are produced in inadequate numbers because of lack of funds for procurement. The 1977 change in Pentagon organization that made the director of defense research and development also responsible for acquisition was a sensible response to this problem, but Congress still addresses separately in its hearings the two spending categories of R&D and procurement.

A number of recent studies suggests that the balance between development and procurement is badly awry. For example, in 1978 an article could state that "The Army faces a huge 'bow wave' in the funding needed to buy 29 major new weapon systems it wants to field over the next five years";(6) by summer 1979 it was clear that the Army would not be allowed to buy anything like the quantity of new equipment that it had planned, although the military requirement had not eased.(7) A 1977 analysis by the quasi-independent Defense Science Board of DOD concluded more generally that too many military research programs were carried into development even though the prospects for production were bound to be low. The board suggested a variety of procedures which would tighten up the decision-making process, and made the explicit suggestion that less funding for R&D might be a reasonable response if the funds could be applied to procurement. Although the focus of this study was on improved procedures within DOD, Congress must inevitably share some responsibility. By looking only at annual appropriations, Congress is likely to neglect the long-range implications of its budget decisions on RDT&E. Through its proclivity for adjusting the budgets and timetables of individual projects, it further exacerbates the problem of program balance.

A still broader congressional oversight that would link the development and procurement of new weapons to military strategy and foreign policy is also missing. Congress still has no mechanism for integrating its review of DOD's budget for new weapons with an analysis of the underlying assumptions about force structure and the aims of U.S. foreign policy.(8) The previously mentioned special hearings held by the R&D subcommittee of the Senate Armed Services Committee are a step in the right direction, but only a modest step. They have required extensive staff work, both by the committee staff and in the Pentagon, but they have not attracted the attention of a large number of senators. Furthermore, witnesses have been restricted to representatives of the Department of Defense. A broader examination would require the involvement of the Committee on Foreign Relations, testimony from the State Department and from the Arms Control and Disarmament Agency, as well as the views of analysts from outside of government. So long as the committee hears only the views and answers of DOD and the military services, the range of questions asked is likely to remain narrowly focused on "which weapons," not "for what purpose."

POSSIBLE REFORMS

What role ought Congress play in the decision process for new weapons? A minimal reply to this question would stress congressional responsibility to study the RDT&E program and approve a budget for it, making recommendations on individual projects only when the Department of Defense has failed to support its case for funding or has made an obvious mistake. Those who support this view argue that Congress cannot match the executive branch in formulating policy because it lacks analytical capability and is too diverse and uncoordinated to speak with one voice.(9) Instead, Congress's responsibility is the classic one of oversight of the program proposed by the Department of Defense. Congress, so the argument goes, can do a better job of oversight by giving less attention to individual projects, concentrating instead on asking the right questions about overall DOD procedures and intent. Improved policy would come about from congressional insistence on improvements in the quality of the DOD's own analysis of programs and from continued congressional monitoring of the management of ongoing development programs.

There are a number of changes in procedures that could enhance congressional performance in this oversight role, including: more disciplined use of studies commissioned from support agencies such as the Congressional Research Service; reduction in the number of overlapping hearings, by greater coordination between the two houses of Congress; procedures for voting funds for longer than one year in order to reduce the budget instability.(10)   These procedural changes and others like them have the advantage of being politically fea- sible.   They satisfy the dictum of Congressman Les Aspin that "Congress is most comfortable dealing procedurally with national security matters; there they are the experts."(11)

More substantial changes will be necessary if Congress is to integrate its oversight of military RDT&E with an analysis of overall defense spending in the light of national security objectives.   At present, traditional jurisdictional lines sep- arate the armed services committees from the Committee on International Relations in the House and the Committee on Foreign Relations in the Senate.   Cooperation across these lines will be needed to encourage a broader definition of na- tional security and to illuminate the impacts of decisions on weapons developments and military forces.   Increased utiliza- tion of witnesses from outside DOD and the defense industry would be helpful in giving Congress a broader view of na- tional security.

This group of changes can affect policy outcomes by in- creasing the range of participants and enhancing their access to the policy process.   There is a risk, however, that pro- cedural changes alone will continue to succumb to the weight of long-standing interests, so that the system returns, if not to the previous status quo, to a state in which it operates about as narrowly as before.   Any long-lasting reform of congressional action in the area of military policy must ad- dress the underlying pressures that encourage members of Congress to be shortsighted, to concern themselves with the details of projects that affect their own local districts but not in the broader policy issues, and to be willing to accept without much question the basic assumptions that underlie DOD's programs and budget requests.

Most of the pressures of electoral politics are against reforms in this sort of attitude and behavior.   Nevertheless, there is reason for hope.   First it is clear that procedural and institutional changes do make a difference, even if the difference is less than often claimed.   The addition of the congressional budget committees and the Congressional Budget Office, for example, has served to expand the time horizon of congressional debate by requiring information on projected five-year costs of defense programs.   The requirement for arms control impact statements for new weapons developments has similarly given expression to a broader range of concern than had usually been considered by Congress.   It is true that the effects of these changes have not been as great as their proponents had hoped, but this should not obscure the fact that progress has been made.

The crucial question of incentives emphasizes the need to develop a broader public debate on national security and military programs and to introduce the changes in procedure that would give regular access to alternative voices. The precedent of ABM debate and of the SALT II treaty show that sustained public debate is possible. Indeed, the most substantial reason for hope is the considerable progress that Congress has made in the past two decades in transforming itself into a more effective partner in setting defense policy.

NOTES

(1) For a discussion of this trend see Richard Haas, "Congressional Power: Implications for American Security Policy," Adelphi Paper 153, (London: The International Institute for Strategic Studies, Summer 1979).

(2) See Craig Liske and Barry Rundquist, "The Politics of Weapons Procurement: The Role of Congress," Monograph Series in World Affairs, The Social Science Foundation and Graduate School of International Studies, University of Denver, Vol. 12, 1974-75, p. 69. Senator Stennis is still an influential member of both the Senate Armed Services Committee and the Appropriations Committee.

(3) See the interview with Air Force Deputy Chief of Staff for R&D, Lt. Gen. Thomas Stafford, Armed Forces Journal International, November 1979, p. 36.

(4) Congressman Richard H. Ichord, "Micromanagement: The Congressional Perspective," Armed Forces Journal International, October 1977, p. 24-25.

(5) See, for example, Subcommittee on Research and Development, U.S. Senate Committee on Armed Services, "Fiscal Year 1978 Authorization for Military Procurement, Research and Development," Hearings, Part 9, pp. 6051-6114, 95th Congress, 1st Session (Washington: U.S. Government Printing Office, 1977).

(6) "New Systems Pose Huge 'Bow Wave' for Army Budget," Armed Forces Journal International, June 1979, p. 10.

(7) "Five-Year Budget Curbs Aircraft, Ship Buys," Aviation Week & Space Technology, August 27, 1979, p. 12.

(8) Nancy Bearg and Edwin A. Deagle, Jr., "Congress and the Defense Budget," in John E. Endicott & Roy W. Stafford, Jr., eds., American Defense Policy (Baltimore: The Johns Hopkins University Press, 1977).

(9) See Nancy Bearg and Edwin A. Deagle, Jr., "Congress and the Defense Budget," p. 351.

(10) Richard Haas, "Congressional Power," p. 7.

(11) Congressman Les Aspin, "The Defense Budget and Foreign Policy: The Role of Congress," in Arms, Defense Policy, and Arms Control (Daedalus, Spring 1975), p. 167. (emphasis added)

Glossary of Acronyms

ABM   - antiballistic missile

ACDA   - Arms Control and Disarmament Agency

ASD/I&L   - Assistant Secretary of Defense for Installation and Logistics

ASPR   - Armed Services Procurement Regulations

CNA   - Center for Naval Analysis

DCP   - Decision Coordination Paper

DDR&E   - Director of Defense Research and Engineering

DOD   - Department of Defense

DSARC   - Defense System Acquisition Review Council (Advisory Council)

DT&E   - Development test and evaluation

FYDP   - Five Year Defense Plan

GAO   - General Accounting Office

GOCO   - Government-owned company-operated organizations

GPS   - Global Positioning System

ICBM   - intercontinental ballistic missile

IDA   - Institute for Defense Analysis

IOC   - initial operational capability

IR&D   - independent research and development

IR&D/B&P   - independent research and development and bid and proposal

IOC	- initial operational capability
IR&D	- independent research and development
IR&D/B&P	- independent research and development and bid and proposal
JCS	- Joint Chiefs of Staff
MENS	- mission element need statement
MIC	- Military-Industrial Commission (Soviet)
MIRV	- multiple, independently-targetable reentry vehicle (multiple warhead)
MOD	- Ministry of Defense (Soviet)
NATO	- North Atlantic Treaty Organization
NSC	- National Security Council
OFPP	- Office of Federal Procurement Policy
OMB	- Office of Management and Budget
OSD	- Office of the Secretary of Defense
OT&E	- operational test and evaluation
PPBS	- Planning, Programming, Budgeting System
R&D	- research and development
RDT&E	- research, development, test and evaluation
SALT	- Strategic Arms Limitation Talks
SPO	- Special Projects Office
SST	- supersonic transport
TPPC	- total package procurement concept
TTZ	- Tactical-Technical Instruction (Soviet)
TU	- technical conditions document (Soviet)
USD/R&E	- Undersecretary for Research and Engineering
V/STOL	- vertical/short take-off and landing

Index

About the Contributors

Edwin A. Deagle, Jr. is Deputy Director, International Relations at the Rockefeller Foundation. He is a West Point graduate, who in addition to his Army career, has served as Executive Assistant to the Director of the Congressional Budget Office and in the Office of Management and Budget.

Alexander Flax is President of the Institute for Defense Analyses, Washington, D.C. Originally an aerospace engineer, he served as Air Force Assistant Secretary for Research and Development under Secretary of Defense McNamara.

Jacques S. Gansler, Vice President of TASC (The Analytic Systems Corporation), served as Deputy Assistant Secretary of Defense for Material Acquisition and is former Vice President of ITT. He is author of the forthcoming book The Defense Industry.

Richard Garwin is IBM Fellow and Science Advisor to the Director of Research at the Thomas J. Watson Research Center of IBM. He is also Professor of Public Policy in the Kennedy School of Government at Harvard University and has served for many years as a consultant to the U.S. Department of Defense.

Noel Gayler holds the rank of Admiral, USN, (Retired). He served in many important posts during his Navy career, including Commander in Chief, Pacific, and Director, National Security Agency. He is currently a member of the Defense Science Board and on the Boards of the Institute for Defense Analyses and Stanford Research International.

David Holloway is Lecturer in Politics, University of Edin-
    burgh, and currently is a Fellow at the Woodrow Wilson
    International Center for Scholars. He is the author of
    numerous articles on the Soviet Union, and a specialist
    in the area of Soviet military R&D.

Alexander Kossiakoff is Director of the Applied Physics Labo-
    ratory, Johns Hopkins University, where he has been
    since World War II. He has contributed to numerous
    studies and committees concerned with weapons develop-
    ment and use.

F. A. Long is Henry R. Luce Professor Emeritus of Cornell
    University and former Director of the Peace Studies Pro-
    gram. He has had a long involvement in national secu-
    rity affairs and arms control and served during 1962-63
    as Assistant Director of the U.S. Arms Control and Dis-
    armament Agency. He is the editor (with George
    Rathjens) of Arms, Defense Policy and Arms Control,
    (1976).

Robert Perry is Senior Social Scientist and Program Director
    for R&D and Acquisition studies, the Rand Corporation.
    He is the author of numerous reports and papers on
    weapons acquisition, R&D policy, and related issues.

Judith Reppy is Senior Research Associate in the Peace
    Studies Program at Cornell University. She is the author
    of several articles on military R&D.